STANDOUT CHARACTERS

How to Write Characters Who Make Readers
Laugh, Cry, and Turn the Next Page

Mary Lynn Mercer

ISBN: 0692680691
ISBN-13: 978-0692680698

Cover images copyright: kentoh / Shutterstock.com. Used under license.

Book cover design by: Mary L. Mercer 2014

"Port Credit" font by Ray Larabie. "Phosphate" font by Steve Jackaman. "Futura" font by Paul Renner. "Antonio" font by Vernon Adams. "Avenir" and "Avenir Next Condensed" fonts by Adrian Frutiger. "Simonetta" font by Brownfox. "Vollkorn" font by Friedrich Althausen. Used under license.

Previously published as *Standout Characters: How to Forge an Emotional Bond with Readers*.

About the Author

Mary Lynn Mercer's nonfiction books, *Story Bones: How to X-Ray Any Novel for Plot, Conflict, and Character* and *The Midpoint: How to Write the Central Turning Point with Emotion, Tension, & Depth,* hit #1 on Amazon's paid Kindle TV Screenwriting bestsellers list. An experienced national contest judge, avid reader, and movie buff, she enjoys applying creative tools gleaned from years of study and pleasure reading to her own writing. For information on other and future releases, please visit her website at *MaryMercer.weebly.com.*

ALSO BY MARY L. MERCER:

Story Bones: How to X-Ray Any Novel for Plot, Conflict, and Character

The Midpoint: How to Write the Central Turning Point with Emotion, Tension, & Depth

STANDOUT CHARACTERS

PRAISE FOR *STORY BONES*:

"One of the best crafting books I've ever read. What a fantastic book! I love it! Everybody needs to check out Mary's book ASAP."
– Carol A. Hughes, writer/director/producer, creator of the *Deep Story* writing method

For Mom

Table of Contents

Chapter One

It's All About Relationship

Scarlett O'Hara.

Sherlock Holmes.

Bond. James Bond.

All these characters come from very different, very famous stories. All transcended their stories to achieve the type of name recognition enjoyed today by Hollywood's hottest celebrities and Billboard's biggest sensations.

Hints like Margaret Mitchell or *Gone With the Wind* are unnecessary to conjure the associated images of unrequited passion and lifelong devotion against a backdrop of cultural genocide. Likewise Sir Arthur Conan Doyle's brilliant detective lives on, even reimagined for contemporary times, long after the passing of his creator. And the West's favorite spy scarcely ages on page or screen over sixty years since first saving the free world in Ian Fleming's *Casino Royale*.

Few protagonists are deliberately designed to blend into the background or alienate readers. Usually characters painted with a colorless brush are crafted to provoke readers into an objective evaluation of themselves or society as a whole. While Winston Smith is hardly a name that pops vividly to mind, who can forget Big Brother in George

Orwell's *1984*? It's the story, not the character, that continues to haunt generations of readers.

Too many other protagonists unintentionally fall into the great chasm of forgettability in-between. Neither crafted like Scarlett to evoke sweeping emotions or like Winston to point readers toward larger concepts, these unfortunate characters are fated at best for the bargain table at library sales.

So what makes the difference? Why does one character burn bright in a reader's imagination and another lie fallow on the page?

The key is *relationship*, specifically the relationship between the character and the reader. It's a unique emotional bond capable of developing between a flesh-and-blood person holding a book or watching a movie and the imaginary character on the page or screen.

Back in 1956 Donald Horton and Richard Wohl wrote an academic paper introducing their theory of parasocial relationships. Since then there's been numerous studies conducted by leading universities and scientific institutes adding to their findings about how audiences emotionally interact with media. Basically, viewers or readers, while understanding the difference between reality and fantasy, nevertheless experience real emotional attachments to characters on the page or screen. They care about what happens to them like they would a good neighbor, a close friend, or a family member, and may even feel grief when a favorite character is written out of a series or the show is cancelled. This is the result of the character's values, behavior, and personality becoming so real to the audience emotionally that spending time with that fictional person satisfies the universal human craving for companionship and belonging. Particularly vivid characters can even assume the status of role models and increase the audience's sense of self-esteem.

After spending over four hours watching Scarlett O'Hara pine for Ashley or a thousand-plus pages reading about her twisting Rhett up into knots, who doesn't feel as though they've lived with her? Love her or hate her, we've invested time and attention in her. She's become a part of our lives, at least emotionally.

And so has every other standout character I can think of.

You know the kind—the ones you wish you could've written yourself. The kind who inspire reader comments on Amazon like: "When the story ended, I missed these characters so much I went back and re-read the book." "I feel like I know these characters as well as my own family." "The characters are so real, I can't wait for the next book." Go ahead and think of the characters that stepped out of their stories to live in your imagination long after you closed the book or the movie credits rolled.

List the top five that come to mind.

Strong parasocial relationships with vivid characters motivate readers to finish a book, or keep reading until the wee hours of the morning on a weeknight, or rush out to buy the next installment in a series. It's also the essential engine driving the resurgent and exploding popularity of serial storytelling in novels and films worldwide. For example, Korean serials (or "Kdramas"), which specialize in telling complete and contained stories in approximately sixteen to thirty episodes, have taken the world by storm. One Kdrama subscription service boasts that its multicultural membership watch over three times more hours per month than Netflix's and Hulu's members combined. And one popular Kdrama serial accumulated over two billion views online within its first year of release.

Obviously there are lots of good stories out there that entertain the reader until "The End," and then the relationship is over with nary a twinge. Readers forget and move on to the next book or movie.

Really great stories live on with readers long after "The End," and the reason for that is the reader's emotional bond with the characters. It's the promise of renewing that special relationship or striking up a similarly satisfying one that generates word of mouth publicity and develops a devoted readership. A so-called high-concept or fresh twist on a popular genre might initially snag a reader's attention, but it's the characters who land a book on the high-value keeper shelf.

Therefore the savvy writer is like a gardener who understands that their work isn't over when they dig out a well-structured plot and plant three-dimensional characters. They still need to water the garden with proven techniques designed to grow an emotional connection between the characters and readers.

A lot of skilled writers work diligently at plot and characterization, but mistakenly believe they must leave the emotional bond, like the promise of rain, up to chance. This approach guarantees hit-or-miss results. Some books will sell well and resonate with readers, while others may bear few sales or none at all. This frustrating cycle of lean and plenty engenders self-doubt, and can eventually paralyze the creative process.

But you don't need to remain a victim of chance.

The power to move a reader's emotions is within your grasp. Specific techniques exist to craft that special relationship on the page. Imagine your fingertips flying across the keyboard, confidently evoking curiosity, tension, and excitement in your reader at will.

Remember that list you made a little while ago? Add one more name to it—the name of your character, right at the top.

Chapter Two

Quick and Simple Characterization

Although intrinsically related, creating a three-dimensional character on the page is a different goal and a different process than emotionally bonding that character with readers. This is an important distinction, because it is entirely possible to successfully create a realistic character who nevertheless leaves readers cold and untouched. Several very good books have already been written about characterization techniques, and are recommended at the conclusion of this chapter.

Of course before a reader can invest in a character, there must first be a character to invest in. So here are a few quick and simple tips to get you started building a character from the ground up.

FINDING THE PIECES

Assuming you already have an idea in mind for a story, consider the character's dramatic role or function. This is similar to the initial steps in putting together a puzzle, such as identifying whether it's going to be a picture of a lake, a city skyline, kids playing with a dog, etc. If you have some idea of the ultimate design, you'll enjoy the process a lot more.

So are you constructing a protagonist, a villain, a romantic interest, a mentor, or a sidekick? Determining the character's role early on will help fill in the blanks later when coloring in the details of their characterization. For example, in *While You Were Sleeping* the protagonist is a natural girl-next-door type while her fiancé's scary girlfriend (a minor supporting character) is a plastic-surgery poster-girl. The differences between these two characters are heavily informed by their roles and the thematic issues in the story.

Next, consider what you know of the plot, especially key events. Does it require the character look or behave a certain way? An example is Bilbo Baggins in J.R.R. Tolkien's *The Hobbit*, whose small size and furry hobbit feet get him mistaken for a troll's dinner but also enable him to slip stealthily out of many dangerous situations.

Now it's time to define the basic parameters of the character. These are like positioning the corner pieces of the puzzle. They aren't the whole picture by a long shot, but once you know the character's boundaries, it's so much easier to arrange the details later.

Corner Piece #1 — When you meet someone for the first time, what do you notice first? Probably whether they are **male or female**. Seems pretty basic, I know, but don't overlook the obvious difference this makes to the character's outlook on life, position in society, and even dialogue quirks.

Most women are aware of their bodies in different ways than men, and this applies to more than explicit love scenes. Just ask any medical professional which gender is generally able to specifically describe symptoms. Right, it's women. Men are notorious about glossing over or ignoring health concerns. Size and strength attributes commonly associated with gender also informs the person's sense of responsibility toward the safety of themselves and others.

Whole books have been written detailing the differences in communication styles and speech patterns between men and women. Men tend to interrupt more, whereas women tend to reflexively apologize even when not at fault. Men brag about themselves. Women take things personally and hold grudges longer.

Corner Piece #2 — The next thing you might notice about someone is their **age**. Ordinarily children and young adults live life at warp speed, still learning to associate actions with consequences. Older people, extremely conscious of potential consequences to health or security, often slow down to avoid mistakes.

Corner Piece #3 — If you're acquainted with a person more than a few minutes, usually you learn something about their **job** or **hobbies**. Think beyond what they do to make a living. What kind of tasks are they suited for? What does the character dedicate the majority of their time and energy to when it's left up to them?

Corner Piece #4 — Notice that I didn't mention **appearance** first, such as hair, skin, eyes, clothes, etc. Detailing how a person looks only scratches the surface of characterization, *unless* it's vital to the plot or expresses a personal choice revealing the character's inner life. Then a character's appearance becomes important because it points not to the fashionable brand name label in their suit or the rip in their faded jeans, but rather to their motivations, conflicts, and goals.

Even descriptions of the character's face can provide readers with subtle clues to habitual attitude and behavior patterns. That's because people's longterm emotional states release chemicals and hormones influencing bone structure and muscle formation. Also, if the character's face sports irregularities due to injury, substance abuse, or reconstructive surgery, for example, these details telegraph to readers important aspects of the character's values, background, or self-worth.

In *Gone with the Wind,* Margaret Mitchell devotes not only the first line of the book, but the entire first page to describing her heroine's appearance. Even at sixteen, Scarlett O'Hara is a confident vixen of the most virtuous order. The writer paints a detailed image of facial features obliquely suggesting an intelligent and deceitful nature that thrives on challenges. Her upward-slanting eyebrows subliminally foreshadow an iron will unintimidated by obstacles. It's clear that regardless of her well-mannered trappings, Scarlett's eyes are truly the windows into her sensual, stubborn, and tempestuous soul. Describing her appearance is essential to convincing the reader this young woman can bring men to their knees.

By contrast, John D. MacDonald didn't write a single word of physical description of his iconic hardboiled sleuth Travis McGee until the end of chapter two in *The Deep Blue Good-by*. Even then, it's barely a sketch: "big brown loose-jointed... pale-eyed, wire-haired...knuckly, scar-tissued reject..." Little more was necessary to the story's development, and readers buy into McGee's credibility as a "salvage consultant" without immediately needing to know what he looks like.

Now it's time to connect the four corners with border pieces to provide the picture with shape. Characters who are developed no further than sex, age, job, and appearance rest lightly on the page, suitable for walk-on parts but unable to make an indelible impression on the reader's mind or heart. To assume dimension and emotional depth, the character needs to be equipped with a unique perspective about themselves and their circumstances in life. Individualization occurs primarily through the character's **attitudes** about themselves and others, and the expression of their **values** through freewill choices they make impacting their own lives and others.

Think about the main characters on TV's *Desperate Housewives*. They were all women, all around the same age, all housewives, and pretty much all shared the same socioeconomic class. What made Susan, Lynette, Bree, and Gabrielle unique and individual from one another were their attitudes and values. Which character felt she had to always be the perfect Supermom? Which character valued sexual liberation above fidelity?

Or TV's *Army Wives*. All women, all married, all mothers, and all scrambling to find or maintain their place in the military culture. But one feels like a fish out of water, while another revels in her status as an old pro. One finds a sense of security in her role, while another chafes at the restrictions.

A men-centric example is Lt. Gen. Harold G. Moore (ret.) and Joseph L. Galloway's autobiography *We Were Soldiers Once...and Young*, later made into the movie *We Were Soldiers* (2002) starring Mel Gibson. The main story involves the first American battle of the Vietnam war. The characters on the battlefield are all men, all military, all in overwhelming danger. In that situation it takes more than rank and a salute to make a lieutenant different from a sergeant. The green lieutenant struggles to reconcile conscience with duty, while the grizzled sergeant slides grimly yet comfortably into the familiar rhythms of his third war.

Time to make another list. Establish the general parameters of your character. Write down their—

Sex.

Age.

Job/Hobby.

Appearance.

Now individualize them by noting their *attitudes* and *values* about each area. For example, in H. Rider Haggard's worldwide bestseller *She*, the title character is a powerful sorceress who blatantly uses her sexuality to exert absolute rule over a hidden kingdom. But in Nathaniel Hawthorne's *The Scarlet Letter*, a mistake in moral judgment turns a woman into a lifelong outcast, largely based on her femininity. For one character, her gender role is a source of power, for another character it's a source of shame and disgrace. Two totally different attitudes and values expressed by the characters and their respective communities about one common facet of the human condition.

FILLING IN THE PICTURE

Attitudes and values are the result of heredity, upbringing, environment, and life experiences filtered through personality structures. It's like everyone is seeing the world through a different pair of glasses. This explains why four people witnessing the same traffic accident at an intersection can give four very different statements to police, while telling the absolute truth *as they see it*. Or why identical twins growing up in the same home and afforded the same economic and social advantages can lead totally different lives.

The Enneagram is a popular personality resource that's highly useful for writers. It's a valuable tool to understand character motivations, conflicts, strengths, flaws, backstory wounds, and potential character arcs. All of these things contribute to shading one person's glasses a different color than someone else's.

Below are brief descriptions of the nine core personality types. For in-depth exploration of the Enneagram, the following resources are highly recommended: Renee Baron & Elizabeth Wagele's *Are You My Type, Am I Yours?* and Don Richard Riso with Russ Hudson's *Personality Types: Using the Enneagram for Self-Discovery*.

Type One

At their best, Type Ones are incorruptible idealists who are unafraid of self-sacrifice in service to a noble cause. Their innate sense of humanity combined with self-discipline produces an inward understanding they are here for a larger purpose than self-gratification, and that their actions and behavior are capable of making the world a better place. Examples include Atticus Finch in Harper Lee's *To Kill a Mockingbird*, missionary Rose Sayer in C.S. Forester's *The African Queen*, and Marilla Cuthbert in Lucy Maud Montgomery's *Anne of Green Gables*.

At their worst, Type Ones are petty, abusive, controlling tyrants who view everyone around them as morally inferior to themselves. They feel justified denying others the right to independent action and self-determination. To defend themselves against their own hyper-critical thoughts, they demand others agree with them about everything. Examples include Javert in Victor Hugo's *Les Miserables*, Eugenia Wraxton in Georgette Heyer's *The Grand Sophy*, and Nurse Ratched in Ken Kesey's *One Flew Over the Cuckoo's Nest*.

Type Two

At their best, Type Twos are warmly generous nurturers. They instinctively respond to someone in need. Their keen and natural perception usually enables them to deliver exactly the assistance required, with grace and genuine goodwill. Steadfast and unconditional loyalty is a hallmark of their friendly nature. Examples include Dorcas Lane in *Lark Rise to Candleford*, Michael Westen in TV's *Burn Notice*, Jack Travis in Lisa Kleypas's *Smooth-Talking Stranger,* and Sophy Stanton-Lacy in Georgette Heyer's *The Grand Sophy*.

At their worst, Type Twos are possessive manipulators, skilled at the fine art of guilt-tripping others. They can be prone to histrionic displays of martyrdom to garner attention and guarantee they receive proper gratitude for their "sacrifices." A Two's natural sensitivity to others deteriorates into "giving to get," as their fear of being unloved turns them into possessive, clingy parasites. Examples include Annie in Stephen King's *Misery*, Deena in Terry Goodkind's *Wizard's First Rule*, and Angela Lansbury's portrayal of Mrs. Eleanor Shaw Iselin in *The Manchurian Candidate*.

Type Three

At their best, Type Threes are self-motivated achievers who thrive on challenge. They are consummate planners and organizers, adept at whipping an event or project into shape in no time. Indefatigable and optimistic, their can-do spirit is an inspiration to everyone around them. Examples include Audrey fforbes-Hamilton in TV's comedy *To the Manor Born*, Meredith Sinclair in Sara Mitchell's historical romance *Shenandoah Home*, and Tom Cruise's portrayal of Mitch McDeere in *The Firm*.

At their worst, Type Threes are opportunistic egotists willing to lie, cheat, and steal to secure the top spot, and proud of it. Bossy, they boldly elbow others out of the way to grab the spotlight. They are vain in the extreme, but also cunningly able to instantaneously adapt their appearance and behavior to curry favor. Examples include Peter Callaghan in *While You Were Sleeping*, Lady Nadia in Patricia Veryan's *Ask Me No Questions*, and Don Draper in TV's *Mad Men*.

Type Four

At their best, Type Fours are compassionate individualists, dedicated to making a positive contribution in the world. Their emotional intensity and perceptiveness energize an affinity for creative expression. Dedicated to authenticity, they disdain phoniness in themselves or others, and usually enjoy a natural immunity to peer pressure. Examples include Chuck Bartowski in TV's spy spoof *Chuck*, Lucy Moderatz in *While You Were Sleeping*, and Anne Shirley in Lucy Maud Montgomery's *Anne of Green Gables*.

At their worst, Type Fours are self-entitled elitists, too special for their own good. Their extreme mood swings and neediness are emotionally fatiguing to those around them. They get so caught up in being true to themselves, that they forget to engage with the world around them, and languish their lives away envying others who inevitably seem happier and more fulfilled than themselves. Examples include the Joker in *The Dark Knight*, the Phantom in *The Phantom of the Opera*, and Blanche DuBois in Tennessee Williams' *A Streetcar Named Desire*.

Type Five

At their best, Type Fives are resourceful pioneers, capable of harnessing incredible focus to achieve objective outcomes and solutions. Combining deep knowledge with visionary foresight, they are the valued brain trust of any group or society they belong to. Curiosity can drive them to great feats of courage. Hidden wells of deep emotion make them capable of incredible loyalty and focus in relationships. Examples include Sherlock Holmes in Sir Arthur Conan Doyle's *The Hound of the Baskervilles*, Michael Scofield in TV's *Prison Break*, Chloe O'Brien in TV's *24*, and Arthur Chipping in James Hilton's *Goodbye, Mr. Chips*.

At their worst, Type Fives are arrogant eccentrics who derive perverse satisfaction from delivering incisive put-downs of those they deem mentally inferior. They are emotionally and materially stingy, committed to living their lives with as minimal emotional involvement or physical needs as possible. They may even adopt an anarchistic worldview as a type of psychological defense against the world's overwhelming sensory demands. Examples include Anthony Hopkins' portrayal of Hannibal Lecter in *The Silence of the Lambs*, Ebenezer Scrooge in Charles Dickens' *A Christmas Carol*, and Van Heerden in Edgar Wallace's *The Green Rust*.

Type Six

At their best, Type Sixes are courageous and loyal. "Be Prepared," is their favorite motto, and they can always be trusted to have their friends' backs whenever the chips are down. Adept at counting the costs of any endeavor, they are skilled at instantaneously assessing the stakes of any situation. Examples include Felix in TV's *Orphan Black*, Bruce Wayne in Christopher Nolan's *Batman* trilogy, and Deputy Barney Fife in TV's *The Andy Griffith Show*.

At their worst, Type Sixes are cruel paranoiacs. Eaten up with fear about their own survival, they make a devil's bargain with whomever guarantees their safety. Their hallmark is a barbed tongue they keep razor sharp by applying liberally to anyone within striking distance. Sniveling and cowardly on one hand, they can also be compulsive daredevils on the other, but either way their eye is always on what they fear most. Examples include Rumplestiltskin in TV's *Once Upon a Time*, Captain Queeg in Herman Wouk's *The Caine Mutiny*, and Norman Bates in *Psycho*.

Type Seven

At their best, Type Sevens are enthusiastic adventurers gamboling merrily through life and brightening the days of everyone around them. For all their imagination and fun-loving ways, however, they are also gifted with practical foresight which usually safeguards them from clambering aboard any bandwagons headed over a cliff. Egalitarian, they are sublimely unconscious of artificial class or hierarchal boundaries, and respect differences rather than impose them. Examples include Peter Pan in J.M. Barrie's *Peter Pan*, Molly MacDonald in TV's *Monarch of the Glen*, and Charlie Haslemere in TV's *The Duchess of Duke Street*.

At their worst, Type Sevens are self-centered wastrels, compelled to run off on an impulsive tangent at the moment others need them most. When the going gets tough, the only thing they can be relied on is to head for greener pastures. Insatiable narcissism hardens them until they are incapable of either fidelity or contentment. Examples include John Willoughby in Jane Austen's *Sense and Sensibility,* Diana Scott in *Darling,* and Paul Newman's portrayal of Hud Bannon in *Hud.*

Type Eight

At their best, Type Eights are tenacious defenders of justice and protectors of the weak. Without trying, they exude an aura of raw power and confidence wherever they go. Nothing gives them greater pleasure than empowering someone who's been pushed down to stand on their own two feet again. They pride themselves for their innate honesty and lack of pretense, and have a nose for sniffing out falsehood in others. Examples include Katniss Everdeen in Suzanne Collins' *The Hunger Games,* John Wayne's portrayal of Rooster Cogburn in *True Grit,* Charles Rivenhall in Georgette Heyer's *The Grand Sophy,* Louisa Trotter in TV's *The Duchess of Duke Street,* and Mitch Rapp in the thriller series by Vince Flynn.

At their worst, Type Eights are ruthless dictators who wage a war of personal revenge against anyone who dares challenge their absolute control. Often rude and crude, they revel in abusive confrontation and intimidation designed to strip their opponent down to the bone. They are animals of excess. Enough is never enough, especially if it involves physical stimulation of any kind, such as food, drink, or sex. Examples include Little Bill Daggett in *Unforgiven,* Lee J. Cobb's portrayal of Juror #3 in *12 Angry Men,* Lord Hibbard Green in Patricia Veryan's *A Shadow's Bliss,* and Junior Allen in John D. MacDonald's *The Deep Blue Good-by.*

Type Nine

At their best, Type Nines are patient peacemakers. Blessed with a unique ability to see all sides of a situation at once, they are skilled at healing breaches in relationships or discovering previously unrecognized solutions. The most supportive of friends, they are quick to unselfishly lay aside their own concerns or interests to help someone else fulfill their dream or escape a difficult situation. Examples include Jack Callaghan in *While You Were Sleeping*, Peeta in Suzanne Collins' *The Hunger Games*, Archie MacDonald in TV's *Monarch of the Glen*, Matthew Cuthbert in Lucy Maud Montgomery's *Anne of Green Gables*, and Bilbo Baggins in J.R.R. Tolkien's *The Hobbit.*

At their worst, Type Nines are mulishly passive-aggressive. Indecisive in the extreme, they're so preoccupied with accommodating everyone they wind up pleasing no one by refusing to take any stand. Emotionally neglectful of themselves and others, their relationships stagnate and they live their lives on perpetual pause. What's worse, they don't even care. Examples include Humbert Humbert in Vladimir Nabokov's *Lolita*, Lester Burnham in *American Beauty*, Professor Grady Tripp in *Wonder Boys,* and Richard Bucket in TV's *Keeping Up Appearances.*

Any good personality book can provide you with a plethora of details to choose from when customizing your character, but really all you need is two or three carefully selected traits to create a **primary picture**. Think of it as a candid snapshot, or a photo still from a scene in a movie. The character is captured in the middle of some telling activity, his personality on full display, attitude flashing from his eyes. In real life people are complex, but in fiction convincing characterization is accomplished through focusing the reader's attention on only those elements essential to the immediate story.

For example, in real life Rick may be a successful businessman willing to trade enough shady favors to stay on the good side of corrupt local officials. (Traits: refined, entertaining, comfortable with dark side.) At the same time, he's rattled by the unexpected return of an old flame on the arm of her new fugitive boyfriend. (Traits: passionate, individualist, jealous, cynical.) Simultaneously, he's accepted an unwelcome position of responsibility safeguarding stolen goods for a friend in trouble. (Traits: supportive, empathetic, risk-taker.)

But the writers of *Casablanca* understood that in fiction Rick's story needed focus to prevent confusing the audience. Is his story about overthrowing government corruption? Or is it about reclaiming lost love? Or is it about helping friends in need?

Once the writer settles on what the story's about, then the other areas of Rick's life can be recast as subplots exploring different angles of the same two or three primary traits. Suppose the writer decides the main story is about Rick's learning how to move beyond emotional pain to stand against injustice? The government corruption thread can be tweaked to highlight his individualism. When the authorities threaten his lady love, he takes matters into his own hands. And the stolen goods thread can be tweaked to awaken his latent sensitivity, albeit cynically denied at first, to the cause of the weak and powerless.

A character's flaw originates from their fears and the lies they believe about themselves. It has both psychological and moral components, which means the flaw negatively impacts not only the character themselves (psychological), but also makes them disregard the welfare of others in some way (moral). In the example with Rick, his cynicism isn't only sabotaging his own happiness, it also puts his true love in jeopardy and threatens the cause of global freedom.

Notice that all of Rick's traits aren't negative, even though his flaw is dragging himself and others to a dismal end unless he makes some significant changes in his life. Be careful if the character is the protagonist that their moral strengths always outweigh their moral weaknesses. The majority of a protagonist's traits need to be positive so they've got at least a fighting chance at a satisfying resolution.

Keeping your various plot threads in mind, create a candid snap shot of the character by jotting down three positive traits and one negative trait for your character. Think about how these traits are related or contrast each other thematically. Ironically, the negative trait is often an extreme, unhealthy expression of the character's greatest strength.

FROM IDEA TO PAGE

What transforms personality traits from abstract words or concepts into pictures for the reader? Tags are the tool writers use to externalize the character's inner reality. Jack Bickham in *Writing and Selling Your Novel* says, "A tag is simply an outwardly visible (or hearable) appearance or activity or habit or thing that you hang on the character." (137)

One of the ways minor characters are differentiated from major characters is by their tags. Minor characters have fewer and less meaningful tags than major characters. The protagonist's nearsighted coworker may wear glasses with big, brightly-colored frames, while their neighbor across the street mows his lawn with obsessive compulsion come flood or drought. These tags hint at single personality traits, keeping the characters firmly rooted in the background of the story.

Major characters graced with several personality traits benefit from a more three-dimensional application of identifying labels. Bickham encourages thinking in terms of "tag clusters" for each personality trait. A cluster of tags realistically rounding out a major character include—

Physical details (clothing, jewelry, scars, etc.)

Specific skills (great cook, computer whiz, military training, etc.)

Dialogue patterns ("Golly!" "Well, fiddle dee dee!")

Behaviors (Pollyanna cheerfulness, stealing, racist, etc.)

Quirks (popping bubblegum, whistling, chewing fingernails, etc.).

Tags are a subtle but essential way to "show, don't tell" characterization. So instead of telling the audience Rick is an individualist to the point of being a loner, the writer would come up with two or three tags from each category to demonstrate this trait. For example, refusing to drink with customers is a behavior tag. "I stick my neck out for no one," is a dialogue tag.

Developing a repertoire of trait tags to dip your pen into on a regular basis scene by scene helps guarantee consistent characterization and guards against unintentionally schizophrenic characters. For example, a consistent character with a trait of independence might have dialogue tags that include, "I've got a plan," or "Here's what I'm going to do."

An inconsistent character might tell themselves, *I'm independent. I can take care of myself*, but then wait for others to make decisions or set agendas on their behalf: "Do you have a plan? What should I do next?" The inconsistent tags cancel out the personality trait the writer is attempting to dramatize.

Nothing will break the reader's bond with a character faster than inconsistent characterization. It throws readers so off balance they can't trust where the character's coming from or anticipate where they're heading, thus damaging the story's structural integrity. It's also the chief symptom of Too Stupid to Live syndrome, and results in the reader losing all respect for the character and confidence in the author.

For each trait you chose for your character, add tags for the following categories: physical detail, skill, dialogue, behavior, and quirk. List at least a couple tags per category for each trait. (The quirks category is an exception. Less is more. Too many diminishes the dramatic impact and risks turning the character cartoonish.) Remember, this is the ink well you will draw from to sketch your character on the page. Choose tags that can be shown in action, however small or brief that action might be. Pretend the character is performing in a play onstage, and each tag needs to be something the audience can see or hear.

BACKSTORY

A character without backstory is a character without context, a floating island in the stream of the story, unconnected to their world and surroundings. Everyone has a history that contributes to explaining who they are today. Their present circumstances and driving motivations are the fruit of a crop planted sometime in the past, possibly years or even generations before the story started.

The trick, of course, is to select specific backstory events that support and add interest to the character you've developed thus far. The temptation exists to make a character's backstory more interesting than the actual story. Resist this temptation by making each backstory event answer two questions:

1. Does it contribute to the character's present motivation for his behavior?

2. Does it make the character's current actions more credible?

If the answer to either is *no*, then tweak the backstory until both answers are *yes*, or set the idea aside to use for another character, possibly in a different story.

Reserve significant backstory for major turning points in the story. Make the readers wait and wonder about it until they can't stand not knowing a moment longer. Then set up the big reveal to trigger an important change in the characters' goal or conflict.

On your characterization sheet, write a single paragraph summarizing the character's backstory. Focus on events that shaped the character's fears, beliefs, and worldview. Pay especial attention to important relationships in the character's life, since relationships are often the vehicles for delivering life's most lasting lessons.

NAMES

There's a reason the character Pippilotta Viktualia Rullgardina Kursmynta Efraimsdotter Långstrump is known simply as Pippi Longstocking.

There are several creative considerations for naming your character, but a practical one is how easy is it to type? Go ahead and practice a few times with the character name of your choice. Do the letter combinations flow easily from your fingertips, or do a couple letters keep getting transposed or dropped entirely? Now imagine having to write that name over and over again several hundred times.

Whether you're writing historical, contemporary, futuristic, or fantasy, the character's name should reflect the time period they were born into. This is relatively easy to ascertain for contemporary stories. Check popular songs, celebrities, or cultural icons from around the character's birth year to get the pulse of popular naming trends. For example, a lot of baby Crystals were born during TV's *Dynasty* heyday in the 1980s.

Historical names may require a little more research. Don't stop with a Top Ten list of names for the time period, though. The #1 most popular name on the list only represents a very tiny percentage of babies named. A truer reflection of naming trends can be found in autobiographies and journals of the time. For example, American Civil War diaries reveal the popularity of giving family surnames, particularly the mother's maiden name, as a son or daughter's given Christian name.

Culture and religion exert strong influences over naming practices. The Amish cherish names from the Bible. Catholics are fond of saints' names, and Muslim converts adopt Arabic names.

In some countries, strict government laws guard against any deviation from cultural norms. In Sweden, a government agency approves children's names to make sure aristocratic names remain specially reserved for the aristocracy. Denmark's government has a pre-approved list of 7,000 names to choose from. Forget unisex names in Germany, or middle names in Japan. Brazil is wild about nicknames. And in true Big Brother fashion, communist China requires that a baby's name is simple enough to scan accurately off the tiny tot's national identification card.

Some popular or even unpopular naming associations know no national or ethnic boundaries. Thanks in no small part to the worldwide fame of TV sitcom *I Love Lucy* for over sixty years in syndication, the name Lucy will always carry a different connotation than the name Ethel. On the other hand, a character named Hitler or Stalin is certain to awaken strong and highly negative preconceptions in any audience even remotely aware of their namesakes' crimes against humanity.

Fantasy authors such as J.R.R. Tolkien get to create wonderfully evocative names like Galadriel and Gandalf, and make us smile with names like Bilbo Baggins. But don't kid yourself that fantasy or science fiction writers have it easier than other genre writers. Tolkien created entire functioning alphabets and languages, complete with grammar rules, for the different races in his novels. Even strange or funny names must make sense within the world of the story, whether it's Edgar Rice Burrough's Martian world of Barsoom or a Louis L'Amour western right here on good old planet Earth.

If you don't already know your character's name, choose one now. Keeping your character's background in mind, write the name across the top of the characterization sheet you've developed throughout this chapter. Note any relevant cultural, religious, or historical associations unique to the name. For example, naming a character Melissa (meaning "honey bee") might subliminally reinforce a particularly sweet disposition.

FURTHER READING

Suggestions to deepen your understanding of characterization:

My book, *The Midpoint: How to Write the Central Turning Point with Emotion, Tension, & Depth.* Chapter 2, "Character Flaws." Available in Kindle edition on Amazon and in print wherever books are sold.

Dwight V. Swain's *Creating Characters: How to Build Story People.* Swain's simple, straightforward approach is timeless. Available in Kindle edition on Amazon and in print wherever books are sold.

Bruce Lansky's *The New Baby Name Survey.* Not a traditional baby name book, although meanings are included. Provides insight into how people respond based on first impressions to 2,000 popular and unusual names. Available in used print editions on Amazon and wherever previously owned books are sold.

Jennifer P. Schneider, M.D., Ph.D. & Ron Corn, M.S.W.'s *Understand Yourself, Understand Your Partner: The Essential Enneagram Guide to a Better Relationship.* Available in Kindle edition on Amazon and in print wherever books are sold.

– Chapter Three –

Designing Stories to Capture Reader Empathy

Iconic characters may transcend their stories, but they don't live apart from them in a vacuum. TV's amateur sleuth Jessica Fletcher thrived on murders to solve, and Jack Bauer just wouldn't be the same without terrorists to kill. Scarlett O'Hara is very much a product of her times, and will never be confused with Truman Capote's modern New York City playgirl Holly Golightly.

In every case the character's story was designed to showcase their most emotionally-compelling qualities to best effect. A lot goes into crafting a great novel, but three specific areas offer the writer unique opportunities to build reader empathy directly into the story at the foundational level.

READERS LOVE CHARACTERS WITH A PURPOSE

Maybe not all characters are made to be loved, but the most memorable certainly evoke some kind of strong emotion. In the first season of TV's *Orphan Black*, the protagonist steals cocaine from her abusive drug dealing boyfriend, fakes her own death, steals a suicide victim's identity to empty the woman's bank accounts, and is a lifelong delinquent who hasn't seen her young daughter for nearly a year. Not nice. But she has a powerful empathy ace up her sleeve. She does it all to win a chance at a fresh start with her child.

In *Goal, Motivation, and Conflict: the Building Blocks of Good Fiction*, Debra Dixon says, "In order for the reader to immerse himself in the character's struggles, first the reader has to clearly understand your character's goal." This is what the character wants for the duration of the story, and either achieves or fails to attain by the end. It creates the story's *spine* or *desire line*, a thread of continuity which runs through every scene and holds the story together.

It's no accident that the first thing the audience sees *Orphan Black*'s protagonist doing is desperately trying to reconnect with her child. That goal positions her in the audience's favor *before* they watch her lie, cheat, and steal. It also keeps them connected to her even while her misguided and self-destructive behavior continues to put that same goal in increasing jeopardy.

Readers like characters who want something specific and want it desperately and urgently enough to go after it immediately. *Specific* is key. "World peace" won't work, because characters who philosophize chapter after chapter strain a reader's patience. It would be like watching a quarterback refuse to get off the sidelines and into the game. "A better life" won't work, either, unless the character narrows that down to specifics like a better neighborhood to live in, a good school, a higher-paying/more fulfilling job, etc. And not just any neighborhood, school, or job, either. The neighborhood with the low-crime rate and white picket fences around every house. The school that produced the spelling champion on the news last year. The job with the corner office and a view of the river.

Specifics are important because they allow the reader to clearly ascertain for themselves the worth of the goal, as well as fully appreciate the strength of the opposition trying to prevent the protagonist from achieving their desire. Small-town mayor Phin Tucker in Jennifer Crusie's *Welcome to Temptation* and US presidential candidate William Russell in *The Best Man* are both running for political offices, but what a difference specifics make. Consequently, the nature and strength of the opposition arrayed against them is as different as night from day.

A story goal is always tangible, meaning if readers stood beside the character they could perceive what he wanted with their own five physical senses. In *The Trip to Bountiful*, the elderly protagonist wants to return to the home of her youth. When the audience sees her sitting on the dilapidated porch, they know she's accomplished her goal, albeit a bittersweet one. In *The African Queen*, the main characters want to blow up a German warship. When a storm results in their capture by the same warship, the audience knows they've failed to attain their goal... that is, until the final seconds of the movie. In *While You Were Sleeping*, the protagonist wants to ease her loneliness by joining up with a warm, caring family. When she reveals at the end the deception that brought her into their lives, she sacrifices her goal for a nobler purpose.

Goals engage reader empathy only to the extent the motivating desire behind them is empathetic. Remember, empathy is a separate psychological response from liking someone. In *Writing for Emotional Impact*, Karl Iglesias says, "...we identify with that character and understand his situation, even if we don't agree with it." (53)

Lucy in *While You Were Sleeping* is extremely likable. By contrast, Sarah in *Orphan Black* has alienated almost everyone in her life. But both inspire the audience to identify with their goals because their motivations are grounded in universal human needs. So even if the characters want an outcome that the audience cannot morally wish for them to achieve, the audience will still be interested and emotionally invested in their achieving it because *the audience empathizes with their reason why.*

Iglesias points to Abraham Maslow's Hierarchy of Needs as the touchstone of universal human motivations:

Physiological — Those things vital to immediate physical survival. Example: Jean Valjean in Victor Hugo's *Les Miserables* steals bread because his family is starving to death.

Security — Those things essential to liberty, self-defense, and long term survival. Example: Bruce Wayne in *Batman Begins* turns outlaw vigilante to save Gotham from criminals and corruption.

Social — Relationships that contribute positively to the person's sense of love, affection, and belonging. Example: Lucy in *While You Were Sleeping* will do anything to belong to a warm, caring family.

Esteem — Those things reflecting self-worth and personal significance. Example: Tess in *Working Girl* steals her backstabbing boss's job, clothes, and boyfriend for a chance at claiming the professional esteem she deserves.

Self-actualizing — Those things expressing a person's true self and sense of personal fulfillment. Example: Penny Chenery in *Secretariat* risks her marriage, her family, and her fortune to see her beloved late father's horse realize his destiny.

Write down your character's story-length goal. Think in terms of real and physical. Is it something a reader could witness or touch for themselves if they were in the story world with the character?

Now write down a universal human motivation driving that external goal, and place it in context within the story. How does it relate to the character and their specific circumstances? Refer to Maslow's Hierarchy of Needs for inspiration.

READERS LOVE CHARACTERS WITH A PLAN

"A goal without a plan is just a wish." — Antoine de Saint-Exupéry

A character demonstrates their commitment to their goal when they put their desire into action by coming up with a plan. It doesn't have to be a perfect plan. Usually during the course of the story they travel an internal arc, growing emotionally/morally/psychologically, so often the initial plan they come up with is actually quite flawed. It almost always results in getting them deeper into trouble and farther away from their goal. At some point they'll be forced to adjust or change their plan as they encounter opposition and become increasingly self-aware, but the point is that an active character always has a plan. The only essentials are that it makes sense to them at the time (avoid plans that are Too Stupid to Live, please!), and it makes them proactive in the plot.

It's that *proactive* part that attracts a reader's interest. The story goal gets the quarterback into the game, but it's his plan that gets the ball moving on the field and the fans cheering.

In *Writing Love: Screenwriting Tricks for Authors II*, Alexandra Sokoloff says, "...drama is the constant clashing of a hero/ine's PLAN and an antagonist's, or several antagonists', PLANS... Stating the plan tells us what the CENTRAL ACTION of the story will be." In other words, the character's plan defines the plot.

Don't assume just because the concept of plot is fundamentally basic to storytelling that every story, even those with complex characters, automatically has one. Famed motion picture director Martin Scorsese said of his twentieth feature-length film *The Departed*, which won him his first Director's Guild of America Award (and later his first Academy Award in the same category): "This is the first movie I've done with a plot." It also remains his highest grossing film to date. Having a plot helped connect *The Departed* to audiences in ways that his other critically-acclaimed films could not.

A character with a plan hooks into a reader's sense of expectation by forming a question in the reader's imagination: "Will the protagonist be able to carry out their plan in spite of the opposition arrayed against them?" Nothing that generic, of course. Here are some specific examples:

Die Hard: "Will John McClane be able to rescue his wife and the other hostages in spite of Hans Gruber's murderous team of bank robbers?"

To Kill a Mockingbird: "Will small town attorney Atticus Finch be able to win justice for a falsely accused black man in spite of organized racial prejudice?"

While You Were Sleeping: "Will Lucy be able to pull off the charade that she's a comatose man's fiancee in spite of his brother's suspicions?"

Write down your character's plan for achieving their goal. How is their flaw responsible for the plan failing at a crucial moment? What new and improved plan do they come up with as a result?

Based on your answers, write down the central story question designed to evoke the reader's sense of expectation. "Will [__*protagonist*__] be able to [__*put their plan in action*__] in spite of [__*opposition*__]?"

READERS LOVE CHARACTERS WITH SOMETHING TO LOSE

Readers experience feelings of tension, that edge-of-their-seat grip-the-book-with-both-hands kind of anxiety, when they're made aware of what's at stake for the character. What do they have to gain that they don't already have but desperately and urgently need? What do they have to lose that's too precious to live without?

It's the reason the character won't quit when the going gets tough. It's the ultimate test of who they are inside at their deepest core—what they love, what they hate, what they value. Stakes lay bare a character's deepest motivations, drive them forward through the story even when their brilliant plan falls apart at the seams, and emotionally bonds the reader to the character's decisions.

In *Techniques of the Selling Writer*, Dwight V. Swain says, "Reasons for a character's not quitting fall into two categories: physical situation, and emotional involvement. A high proportion of story people have both." (174)

Stakes derived from physical situations establish for readers the larger context of the story. They often involve people other than the main character. In *Speed*, the lives of a busload of complete strangers are at stake. The same bomber who threatened a small group of strangers in an elevator at the beginning of the story ups the stakes by increasing the number of potential victims. The implication is clear. If he isn't stopped, even more people will face death. In *Casablanca*, the fate of the resistance organization in Europe against the Nazis is at stake. These are nameless, faceless characters who are never introduced, but the larger context of the story becomes clear to the audience. The fate of the free world may hang in the balance.

Violent death or global tyranny may seem like extremely high stakes, but they don't mean much emotionally to readers until they are paired with personal stakes. That's the emotional involvement Swain talked about. "The flamboyant, the spectacular, the cosmic mean less than nothing. Always, always, you *must* measure in terms of the effect the event has in relation to your focal character's feelings and the story question." (Swain 177)

In *Die Hard*, the physical stakes in the plot effect a horde of partying rich corporate executives. The personal stakes, the emotional involvement, is that John McClane's estranged wife is trapped with them. Now pump up the personal stakes higher. She's not only his wife, she's the mother of his two small children. Go higher still. He's flown thousands of miles at Christmas time in an awkward attempt at reconciliation because he still loves her. That's the kind of stakes that tie the character's feelings into the central story question flashing brightly in the audience's mind: "Will John McClane be able to rescue his wife and the other hostages in spite of Hans Gruber's murderous team of bank robbers?"

In *Casablanca*, the physical stakes in the plot effect the European resistance and by extension the entire free world. The personal stakes, the emotional involvement, is that it's not just anyone asking Rick's help getting Victor Lazlo away from the Nazis. It's the love of his life who chose Lazlo over him. Now pump up the personal stakes higher. She's married, so if Rick lets the Nazis take his romantic rival out of the equation, Ilsa goes down with him. Go higher still. Rick and Ilsa are still deeply in love with each other. Now Rick's feelings are engaged, and so are the audience's, who fully understand what the protagonist has to gain or lose from the central story question: "Will Rick help the love of his life escape with Lazlo from the Nazis?"

How do physical and personal stakes work in quieter stories, the kind that don't have bombs and bullets and jackboots storming across the pages? First, match the plot stakes to the kind of story the reader is expecting. In mysteries, suspense, and thrillers, the plot stakes often involve violent death or global catastrophe. While in romances, women's fiction, and young adult, the plot stakes involve day-to-day problems like health issues, job loss, finances, weddings, inheritance, adoption, etc.

For example, in a romantic comedy like *While You Were Sleeping*, Lucy's physical situation involves a case of mistaken identity. If she comes clean about not really being a comatose man's fiancee, the shock might kill a sweet little old lady. There's a whiff of physical death, but it's scaled down appropriately to match the lighthearted story. The personal stakes, the emotional involvement, come from the fact that the family who embraces Lucy to their collective bosom isn't just any random family. They're the family of the man she's been fantasizing about sharing a perfect life with. Now pump up the personal stakes higher. It's Christmas and she's so lonely she can't even sleep at night. Go higher still. The man she falls in love with is her sleeping prince's brother.

To find the personal stakes for the protagonist in your story, mine the character's values and backstory for a defining event that emotionally cuts off their retreat from the physical situation they find themselves in. Often this moment from their past involved a particularly painful loss or moral failure on their part, and the current circumstances offer a chance at redemption. The key is framing this event in terms of a significant relationship. In *Writing for Emotional Impact*, Karl Iglesias says, "Stakes are more compelling when relationships are involved." (54)

The defining event may play a significant part in the current story, such as Rick and Ilsa's ill-fated love affair in Paris told via extended flashback. Or it may be completely unrelated to the main plot, such as the death of Lucy's father mentioned in merely a line or two of dialogue. The point is that an emotional wound delivered by or during the course of the defining event can only be redeemed or healed by the protagonist's taking decisive action in the story now and risking all.

As the physical and especially the emotional stakes continue to rise in the story, the character is forced to adapt and change their response to events. In other words, they take an internal journey and change on the inside—the way they treat others, the way they think, what they value. As the reader watches these changes develop across the pages, anticipation builds. Curiosity percolates about how the character will change next.

Internal change is most effectively externalized in present day relationships that are central to the protagonist's happiness or success. How does the audience know Rick has rediscovered his lost idealism? Through his relationship with Ilsa, the character who best personifies the stakes in the story. After all, she's the one who will suffer the worst should he continue to hide his heart in a whiskey bottle.

Using the central story question you wrote down earlier as a guide, write down what is physically at stake in the plot. Remember hope versus fear equals tension. So what is the best thing that could possibly happen to the character? What is the worst thing they're afraid will happen or the most painful thing they could lose?

Now write down what is emotionally at stake for your character personally. What relationship is involved and why is it vitally important to the character? Can you pump up the stakes even higher? Come up with a defining event from the character's past that guarantees they cannot walk away from the present stakes without violating their own values or chance at redemption.

FURTHER READING

Suggestions to deepen your understanding of active character goals and stakes.

Debra Dixon's *GMC: Goal, Motivation, and Conflict*. Available in Kindle edition on Amazon and in print from Gryphon Books for Writers.

Alexandra Sokoloff's *Writing Love: Screenwriting Tricks for Authors II.* Chapter 9: "Plan, Central Question, Central Story Question." Chapter 10: "What's the Plan?" Available in Kindle edition on Amazon.

David Howard's *How to Build a Great Screenplay.* Chapter: "The Creation of Drama." Chapter: "Foundations." Available in Kindle edition on Amazon and in print wherever books are sold.

Chapter Four

Building a Bridge to the Reader's Heart

Stakes rev the character's engines to change, but there remains an essential ingredient to bind them to the reader. This single trait is responsible for building an emotional bridge linking the character on the page with the reader's heart and imagination. All subsequent feelings the reader experiences travel on this bridge. It's the load-bearing foundation of reader empathy and identification. Without it, they couldn't care less how likable, intriguing, or interesting a character is.

It's the one trait that's indispensable to making a character effective as a dramatic construction in the reader's imagination. It's not reserved for only the protagonist, either. While the protagonist drives the story, every character has their own agenda and an important part to play. Every character with more than a bit part needs to pull their weight in the story, otherwise they're dead spots in the reader's imagination. To appreciate the full story experience, the reader needs to be allowed to identify on a basic level with every character.

So what is this magic trait that makes a character effective in the reader's eyes?

The ability to take action despite the danger represented by the stakes. A character cannot be a coward paralyzed by fear. They must keep going forward, even though it means doing it afraid. Feeling the fear doesn't make them a coward. In fact, it often makes a character's effort to take action all the more heroic. An example is Marvin Udall in *As Good As It Gets*, when he pushes past his phobias to ride in a taxi or dine in a new restaurant for the sake of a valued relationship. Or Monk in TV's detective series *Monk*, beset by 312 distinct phobias, who regularly has to screw up his nerve to do just about everything that most people take for granted. Or Zoe in Patricia Veryan's historical romance *Never Doubt I Love*, when "Miss Timidity" herself must face down a conspiracy of ruthless traitors to save her beloved brother's life.

Pluck. Bravery. Heroism. Call it what you please, it's easy to build into every character in the story by following a simple, reliable recipe.

Stakes + Forward Action = Courage.

Dwight V. Swain in *Techniques of the Selling Writer* expounds on the quality of courage essential to characters, and describes four ways a character can demonstrate their courage to readers. However, unless the character is on a self-destructive arc spiraling toward tragedy, I find most popular fiction avoids Swain's fourth way: courting disaster. So here are his top three basic types of forward action a character can attempt.

Readers want to be like characters who are brave enough to **attempt something no one has ever done before**. In *The Right Stuff*, set in the mid-20th Century, no one has ever broken the sound barrier or travelled into outer space and lived to tell about it. In Edgar Rice Burroughs' *The Princess of Mars,* no one has ever travelled to Mars and won the hand of a beautiful Martian princess. In J.R.R. Tolkien's *Lord of the Rings* trilogy, no one has ever resisted the ring's evil long enough to destroy it in Mount Doom. In TV's *The Blacklist*, no criminal uber-mastermind has ever joined forces with a special FBI task force to fight crime.

Readers want to be like characters who are valorous enough to **attempt something few others have ever succeeded at**. In *How to Steal a Million,* few others have stealthily reclaimed a statue from a high-security museum. In *Secretariat*, few others have won horse racing's Triple Crown. In *The African Queen*, only one other person has ever navigated a certain river and few if any civilians have sunk a prized German warship.

Readers want to be like characters who are intrepid enough to **attempt something law, society, or morality prohibit**. In *While You Were Sleeping,* morality and society prohibit the protagonist from engaging in mistaken identity to join a family unit. In Harper Lee's *To Kill a Mockingbird,* the law and society prohibit the protagonist from getting justice for a falsely accused black man. In TV's *Prison Break*, the law prohibits the protagonist from breaking a falsely-convicted death row inmate out of a federal maximum security prison. In William Shakespeare's *Romeo and Juliet,* society and their powerful families prohibit a pair of star-crossed young lovers from achieving their happily-ever-after.

For example in Disney's *Frozen*, all the major characters demonstrate courage on some level:

Elsa attempts something no one has ever done before: trying to conceal and control her magic power to turn natural elements into ice.

Anna attempts something few others have ever succeeded at: trying to survive an unnaturally harsh winter storm and scale an imposing mountain to bring her sister back.

Olaf also attempts something few others have ever succeeded at: trying to rescue his ruined ice business from extinction by guiding and protecting an impulsive, naive princess on a reckless quest.

Hans attempts something law, society, and morality prohibit: trying to marry a princess by any means necessary in defiance of the queen's royal decree.

The dramatic success of the character is not in the attainment of any of these things, but in the sheer guts and determination to try. Each of these three categories of action carry high stakes that probably would paralyze to the point of inertia nine out of ten people in real life. So when a character is courageous enough to take a risk the reader wishes they themselves were brave enough to attempt—the empathy hook is set. The reader *wants* to be like that character, *wants* to experience the heroism of courage, even if it's only in one small area of life.

Once the stakes are raised, the pressure is on the character to fold or hold. "If you faint under pressure, you have no courage" (Proverbs 24:10, TPT). The character must never give up, cave in, or quit—though they will certainly feel pressured and tempted to do so. They may even ultimately fail. No reader has ever withdrawn their empathy from a character for failing, only for quitting.

At the midpoint of the movie version of *Gone With the Wind,* Scarlett feels exhausted and overwhelmed. She doesn't have enough money or food to feed everyone. Corrupt taxing authorities and carpetbaggers are salivating over Tara. For a moment, all she wants is to leave the pressures behind and escape with Ashley to Mexico. But it's only for a moment, an acknowledgement of her human condition and the frailties common to everyone. She soon rallies her courage and seductive wiles to save Tara, trap a wealthy husband, and climb back up to the top of the ladder. She's back in the game.

Imagine if she had actually run off to Mexico with Ashley, and the rest of the story was about the new couple's trials and tribulations south of the border. A different story, yes. As richly compelling? No, because it's easy to bail when the going gets tough. That's why the recipe for courage is Stakes + *Forward* Action. Anyone can quit, or turn and run in the opposite direction. But Scarlett O'Hara isn't just anyone. She's a character who transcends her story because she had the courage to live it all the way through to the hard-won (or lost) end.

Courage is relative to the character and the physical/emotional stakes involved in pursuing their specific goal. For Jack Bauer in TV's *24*, courage means saving his family, friends and country from cunning, ruthless terrorists. But for some people who never have to face bombs or bullets, courage may involve simple things most people take for granted. For George Bailey in *It's a Wonderful Life,* courage means staying in his small home town to help his neighbors stand up to rich tyrant Mr. Potter. For free-spirited novitiate Maria in *The Sound of Music*, courage means leaving the security of the abbey and finding her place in a family with seven orphaned children.

Write down in a single sentence what forward action your protagonist dares attempt that either has *never been done before, few have succeeded at*, or is *prohibited by some authority*. Keep in mind that the more intense the pressure is to give up (think: *stakes*), the more courageous the character will seem for trying anyway.

Now write a similar "courage sentence" for each of the other major characters in the story, such as the mentor, deflector, love interest, etc. Remember to include the antagonist. Even if they are a morally evil villain, their ruthless determination to stop the protagonist is essential to the reader's emotional satisfaction.

– Chapter Five –

Introduction to Rooting Interests

Once the emotional bridge is built connecting a character with readers, the writer can roll out fleets of vehicles delivering specific emotions. Instead of steel and rubber, these vehicles are constructed from the character's every word and deed, no matter how small or seemingly insignificant.

That's why first impressions are important. If a book can be judged by its cover, whether fairly or unfairly, a character is judged by the activity they're engaged in when readers first encounter them on the page. It's never too soon to establish reader empathy. To keep readers turning pages, they must care about who they're reading about.

Likewise, to continue caring about the character, the reader must constantly be given reasons to care—page after page until the end. Bestselling historical romance author Donna MacMeans dubs the secret of this magic connection *rooting interests*. These are simply specific traits that firmly seat the reader in the character's cheering section, like a sports fan urging on their favorite team at the national championships.

At first glance, these rooting interests may appear cliche or too common-sensical to pay serious attention to. Resist the urge to assume they will automatically appear on the pages of your story. Deliberately weaving these traits into the characters in fresh and original ways empowers writers to direct readers' emotions with virtuoso skill.

The effectiveness of these traits isn't limited to only the protagonist, either. Precisely because these traits are so powerful, any character can reap the rewards of reader empathy from them. Keep this in mind when crafting other major or supporting characters.

Sometimes a story requires the brief introduction of a minor character whose role in the story is to suffer a quick and tragic end to dramatize and personalize larger plot stakes. This is an especially common device in action, suspense, and thrillers. To guarantee the reader feels the necessary emotional jolt at the character's loss, the writer needs a quick method of building reader identification. After all, this character is basically a complete stranger to the reader and isn't going to last long enough in the story for the reader to get to know them much better. Two or three rooting interests strategically placed in a scene concerning that character can instantly bond the reader to their imminent fate.

On the flip side, if someone other than the protagonist threatens to take over a story, the solution may be found in rebalancing the distribution of empathy traits among the characters. If a supporting character steals the spotlight, odds are they've accrued more rooting interests than the protagonist. The greatest number should always belong to the main character driving the story.

When readers, reviewers, or editors describe characters as "realistic" or "multi-dimensional," it simply means they responded emotionally to the character in ways that successfully mimicked the human experience. Rooting interests draw empathy traits from three specific areas to create a fully-rendered holographic image of the character within the reader's imagination and heart. In short, they make the character feel real.

While these three areas or "dimensions" of character are intimately connected with one another, each expresses a different facet of the human condition at its most intimate and personal levels:

How others treat us.

How we treat others.

How we treat ourselves.

The first is largely outside the character's control, meaning they're on the receiving end of others' (usually negative) decisions and behaviors, which evoke reader empathy on their behalf. This dimension gives the character the opportunity to prove their mettle by constantly testing their courage to press ahead through hard times and life's unfairness. It maintains the empathy bridge and keeps it strong while simultaneously creating a sense of tension.

The last two are within the character's control, meaning their (usually positive) decisions and behaviors directly evoke reader empathy. These dimensions demonstrate the character's moral and psychological health. By creating a sense of understanding and even admiration, they reassure the reader it's safe to lose themselves in the story and vicariously experience it through this character.

Each of the three categories of rooting interests evoke specific feelings in readers. Draw several traits for your character from each category, but keep in mind genre conventions may encourage a heavier proportion of one over others. For example, Donna MacMeans in her online article "Creating Characters for the Keeper Shelf" notes that "... while touching on rooting interests from all three classifications," bestselling romance authors emphasize how the heroine is treated by others. They comprehend the importance of maintaining that empathy bridge with their readers. As for the hero, these same successful authors highlight his psychological health, which stimulates the feeling of admiration essential to fulfilling the reader's sense of vicariously falling in love.

Don't worry about going overboard, especially with major characters. You can almost never have too many rooting interests. In *The Story Solution* Eric Edson says, "The more... attributes included, the more richness, power and depth you give to the most important character in the movie." (14) They create the small moments in scenes that make the story feel real and the characters come alive to the reader. Those are good things you can never have too much of.

FURTHER READING

The following lists of traits are adapted from **Donna MacMeans**' online article "For Writers: Rooting Interests," and **Karl Iglesias's** book *Writing for Emotional Impact*, both highly recommended resources. For Donna's quick list, please visit her website at http://www.donnamacmeans.com/for-writers-rooting-interests. Iglesias's book is available in Kindle edition on Amazon and in print wherever books are sold.

Chapter Six

How Others Treat the Character

Once an emotional bridge is built connecting a character with the reader, it needs to be maintained. Kind of like dispatching the U.S. Army Corps of Engineers to tighten bolts and keep the traffic flowing uninterrupted. That skilled maintenance crew the writer sends in is the category of rooting interests adept at evoking **tension** in the reader.

A character doesn't have to be John McClane fighting terrorists or Sherlock Holmes solving murders to benefit from this category of rooting interests. Tension is simply that deliciously irresistible urge to find out *what happens next?* It's the same kind of feeling shared by any reader who disregards his or her bedtime to read "just one more page" and instead winds up finishing the book at two or three o'clock in the morning. It's every writer's dream to put that bleary-eyed grin of satisfaction on readers' faces, and these are some of the empathy traits that help accomplish that trick.

Rooting interests that evoke tension are derived from external situations that make it harder for the character to carry out their plan and accomplish their goal. It doesn't matter if their goal is to claim a missing inheritance, as in Susan Elizabeth Phillips' *Ain't She Sweet?* Or aid an exiled lion to overthrow an evil witch and deliver a magical kingdom from perpetual winter, as in C.S. Lewis's *The Lion, the Witch, and the Wardrobe.* Or simply survive a government-sponsored gladiatorial death-match, as in Suzanne Collins' *The Hunger Games*.

All the character needs is a goal and a reasonably logical plan that keeps them active in the story. Then find any way you can to make things go wrong. In *Writing with Emotion, Tension, and Conflict*, Cheryl St. John says, "Tension is always about a questionable outcome." (152) So use the traits in this group to throw the success of the character's plan into as much doubt as possible.

This is the domain of the underdog and the victim, where Murphy's Law reigns supreme. The quick and reliable recipe for creating tension can be summed up in one word: T-R-O-U-B-L-E. But trouble is about more than just showing the reader a universally recognizable situation that places the character at a distinct disadvantage. Trouble only hooks into the reader's empathy when it's paired with emotional consequences.

It's the emotional consequences that are key to these traits actually evoking tension in the reader. Remember the personal or emotional stakes you developed for the character earlier? They pay off exponentially here when the odds are stacked even further against the character in ways small and large.

To properly set up tension, make trouble personal to the character. Ramp up the emotional intensity by tying it directly to a wound or ghost from the character's past. An example is Sgt. Al Powell (Reginald Veljohnson) in *Die Hard*. His backstory involves being demoted after mistakenly shooting an unarmed kid. His present job involves a sleepy patrol route, where he's unlikely to need the weapon he's been unable to draw since the accident. At the end of the story, McClane has apparently wiped out all the bad guys and is staggering off to his happily-ever-after (until the sequel) with his wife. Suddenly one of the minor bad guys with a grudge pops up to shoot him, and the only one in a position to take action is Sgt. Powell. The audience's sense of tension spikes because they know the emotionally-wounding event from his backstory directly conflicts with the present problem. Will he—*can he*—shoot the bad guy? His instinctive reaction saves his friend's life and completes his own character arc.

Trouble also needs to be strongly tied to the character's internal goals. In *The Fire in Fiction,* Donald Maass says tension "comes from *emotions* and not just any old emotions but *conflicting emotions.*" (190) The more trouble the character's in, the closer they examine their real reasons for hanging in there and toughing it out. An example is Deanna Dodson's historical romance *In Honor Bound*, where the hero's first wife is murdered (backstory wound) to clear the way for an arranged marriage to the heroine, but in his heart he remains defiant. His internal goal is to remain emotionally faithful to his first wife by refusing to love his second. Trouble arises every time his coldness and aloofness hurts his sweet young bride, whom he knows is an innocent pawn in larger political schemes, and causes him to regret the pain his internal goal causes others.

This is the essence of internal conflict. A character wants two mutually incompatible things at the same time, and can't have both. They must choose one or the other. In Dodson's story, the hero wants to be emotionally loyal to his first wife and defy the will of her murderers, while *at the same time* he wants to be fair to his second wife, who is another innocent caught in the villain's web. When a character experiences internal conflict about the external situation that just made their life so much worse, it generates a sensation of tension in the reader.

What is the reader tense about? What happens next—the character's anticipated response. Will they zig or will they zag to get around this new bump in the road? The only certainty is they must change course or direction. That's how the character advances the story and grows. But change is never a smooth, easy path. Sometimes the character takes one step forward, only to allow fear, anger, or desperation to drive them two steps back. Which sets the reader's emotional pendulum careening between hope and fear, elevating their tension even higher.

Kicking a character when they're down also places them in an inferior position to the reader. This triggers the reader's protective instincts, and invites them to champion the character's cause. It's the David versus Goliath syndrome. No one cares about the giant warrior with everything in his favor. They care about the shepherd boy who's about to get squashed into jelly.

These are the kind of traits that heavily accessorize most successful romance heroines. Gender politics aside, readers resonate with heroines who have it rough. They long to identify with tough survivors determinedly striving toward a tiny flame at the end of a long, dark tunnel. Television networks like Lifetime have built entire audiences by specializing in women-in-jeopardy stories. "Rejoice not against me, O mine enemy: when I fall, I shall arise; when I sit in darkness, the LORD shall be a light unto me" (Micah 7:8, KJV).

That said, it's important to keep the character an active participant in their own life. Find the hidden strength within their weakness or vulnerability. What doesn't kill them *must* make them stronger, both for the story's sake and the reader's. It's downright essential if that character is the protagonist of the story.

Any of the following Tension Traits may be used as individual moments within a scene or as larger plot elements drawn out over a sequence or more. All are customizable to whatever kind of story you're writing. For example, in *While You Were Sleeping* physical jeopardy is played for comedy when Lucy jumps in front of an onrushing train to save a handsome stranger. In *The Bourne Identity* physical jeopardy is played for thrills every time the amnesiac hero pulls off a death-defying stunt. In *Saving Private Ryan* physical jeopardy is played deadly serious as the soldier-heroes storm Omaha Beach on D-Day.

WORKS FOR ANY CHARACTER

The following Tension Traits are so scorchingly powerful that even one on the page can instinctively quicken an immediate feeling of irresistible tension in the reader. This is true regardless if the character involved is a likable protagonist, a vile villain, or a walk-on character.

Injustice and Mistreatment — Put someone in power over the character, and then let that someone abuse their power so that the character unfairly suffers. The greater the injustice to the character, especially if it's combined with physical violence or emotional cruelty, the more potent the reader identification with the victim. Whether it's a prank, a bully's fist, social bigotry, a government cover up, media smear campaign, theft of goods/credit/reputation, or false accusation, this trait is the defining essence of victims and underdogs across all genres. But it also works great to give readers a rooting interest in characters who seemingly have it all, with power of their own, but are incapable of defending themselves in one specific area of vulnerability. The tension escalates even higher if someone else's fate is attached to the character's, so that if they go down by reason of the injustice, others they care about will be dragged down with them.

Secrets — Any secret, no matter how large or small, focuses the reader's attention on whatever might betray the secret or keep it concealed a little while longer. The reader's rooting interest is attached not necessarily to the person with the secret, but rather to the person with the highest personal stakes at risk. Who has the most to lose should the secret be exposed? Who will potentially suffer the greatest loss, hurt, embarrassment, etc.? Sometimes it's the secret-keeper, while other times it's the person the secret is kept from. If readers only know a secret exists and who it's withheld from, but are not privy to the details, it draws them closer to the story, examining events and characters for clues to what's hidden and whom it will impact the most. On the other hand, if reader are let in on all the juicy details, in essence they become co-conspirators with the character.

Repressed Emotional Pain or Longing — Set up this trait early in the character's development, then coax it onto the page by exploring the character's personal stakes in the outcome. Remember, personal stakes are derived from deeply personal yearnings for something the character does not yet possess or is too dear to lose. Yearnings focus on universal needs, such as approval, significance, independence, etc., and the lack thereof inflicts lasting emotional pain in the form of backstory wounds. The character may or may not have suffered a classically tragic past depriving them of kin and home. They might have grown up with every luxury. What matters is connecting the character's personal stakes to resolving their backstory wound, so that every action in the present is motivated by that yearning for something to assuage the old pain. This is a particularly powerful Tension Trait that in combination with other rooting interests (such as regret) can help redeem a character in a reader's esteem from some pretty wretched behavior. However, just because the character has some old scars that never healed doesn't give them license to whine about it. Instead, they suppress the emotional pain in order to make decisions, take action, and drive the story forward.

Weakness and Vulnerability — This is often set up by dangling a carrot almost within the character's reach. Something they intensely yearn for seems to be theirs at last, but then is abruptly denied them or cruelly revealed as an illusion. The whiplash contrast between hope and loss can make them lose their grip on the protective shield they habitually hold in front of their deepest, most sincerest feelings. In that moment, before they can recover their poise, they are vulnerable to the deadliest blow of all—a broken heart. When choosing the carrot to dangle, pick carefully. Broken hearts are serious business, effecting a person's will to live. If a character is in jeopardy of suffering a genuine broken heart over something trivial, such as a supposed friend's catty remark or a scratch on a new car, the reader will recoil at their shallowness. Instead, make the character's yearning universal to readers but personal to the character. The key is to show unmistakable glimpses of the character's suffering, even while he flounders desperately and scrambles awkwardly to tug his emotional armor back into place before someone sees.

Forbidden or Unrequited Love — It takes more than a crush, raging lust, or even obsession to pull off this trait. This is the realm of soul mates and the type of true love that will last as long as the sun and the moon endure. Alas, outside forces (law, society, religion, family, friendships, etc.) oppose their union, and the most the character has reason to hope for is to be there for the beloved should they ever need help. But since when has love had much to do with reason? With such a prize at stake, hope can't resist snatching at the faintest encouragement of realizing love's fondest dream. So this trait comes tantalizingly fraught with lingering looks, stolen caresses, secret rendezvous, and noble sacrifices.

WORKS FOR MOST CHARACTERS

The following Tension Traits are reliable stimulators of tension in the reader when they are placed in the context of emotional and moral stakes effecting the character's important relationships.

Injury, Poison, Illness, or Handicap — Getting injured or poisoned, especially if it's extreme enough to require medical attention, makes the character vulnerable. Since few characters include getting seriously hurt in their plan, it usually represents a dire setback to accomplishing their goal. The reader not only feels sorry for the character's pain, but fears any enemies will seize the opportunity to strike a deadly blow. Long term health issues such as physical or mental handicaps, deformities, and diseases also earn extra empathy from readers. Addictions, provided the suffering they cause is primarily directed toward the character himself more so than others, can also work. (An exception is any addiction involving repeatedly causing others pain and suffering in the story's present day. Then the addict becomes the perpetrator and the reader's pity shifts to the other character as the victim.) Phobias can be just as debilitating as any physical ailment. Poverty and financial hardship can also handicap a character from not only fulfilling dreams but from taking care of basic necessities of life. The key to this trait is never let the character whine about their suffering; give the reader room to feel for them. Then heighten tension by focusing on how this trait traps the character in a bad situation and makes it worse.

Physical Jeopardy — Nearly every James Bond film begins with a death-defying stunt that puts the protagonist's life in danger. It's the kind of hook that never fails to grip the audience's attention with bated breath as they wonder how the character can possibly survive. This rooting interest isn't the exclusive purview of big set pieces and adventure novels, either. It's a great and effective way to highlight even a seemingly ordinary character's capacity for bravery and heroism. But it's the hard choices motivating the character to step into harm's way that energize this rooting interest with real suspense. The highest stakes and hardest choices of all involve the moral dilemmas surrounding relationships with others. Even the most hellacious physical jeopardy imaginable will fall flat with readers unless it is shaped by the character's internal motivations and inner needs. The real tension in physical jeopardy is found in the emotional stakes involved.

Loss and Loneliness — The loss could be the result of death, abduction, mental illness, physical incapacity, or callous neglect. The loss is even more acute if the character is blamed for it or blames himself. The more personal the loss, the greater the emotional impact on both the character and the reader. That's why it often involves lovers, family, or the kind of friends who are closer than a brother. This goes beyond companionship. This is about fracturing the character's sense of wholeness within themselves. The loss and resulting loneliness is so great that it breaks their ability to fulfill their ambitions, dreams, or destiny and move forward along their character arc. Maybe they go through the motions of living or even achieve a kind of public success in life, but they're held back from attempting what really matters to them.

Tells the Truth, but is Not Believed — What will happen if the character is not believed? Who else—besides the character telling the truth—will suffer emotionally or physically because the character is falsely judged a liar? The person who disbelieves the character needs a solid and credible reason to think they're not telling the truth. Often someone seeking vengeance or unfair advantage deliberately and pre-emptively prejudices the unwitting person against the character. But sometimes a character's own behavior or circumstances are enough to cast a shadow of doubt upon their veracity or at least their credibility. Perhaps they've been heavily medicated or recovering from head trauma, or have an obvious motivation to lie, or have cried wolf before. Maybe they're caught in a compromising position and are innocent, but not from lack of desire to succumb to temptation. Combine this trait with a powerful secret for an extra jolt of tension: the character tells a Cliff Notes version of the truth, but because they can't reveal the whole truth without betraying the secret, is not believed.

Blackmailed, Pressured, or Conspired Against — The character is deeply committed to a certain course of action, but someone else does whatever it takes to bend the character to their will. The character wonders who's on their side, whom can they trust, as supposed allies and enemies are subverted or shift sides altogether. To expand the stakes, make the character's decision to stand, bend, or break impact not only their own destiny by also the fate of someone they hold dear. If the conspirators include people whom the character has a justifiable expectation of loyalty from or people they naturally desire to please—lovers, family, friends—then internal conflict is unavoidable and tension runs high.

WORKS FOR SOME CHARACTERS, BUT NOT OTHERS

The efficacy of the following Tension Traits depends heavily on the nature of the character and the specific circumstances involved in order to create tension in the reader. When applied to appealing characters, they evoke worry and apprehension, but when applied to characters who deserve a comeuppance, readers are likely to feel it's justice.

Abandonment and Betrayal — Being left completely alone compels the character to make some hard choices. Ironically for the character, losing all hope of support or rescue from a trusted outside source is often exactly what they need to compel them to face the internal flaws and weaknesses holding them back. Children who are orphaned or otherwise abandoned tug particularly strongly on readers' heartstrings. Charles Dickens and Hesba Stretton built world-renowned careers around urchin characters abandoned and rejected by family or society. Emotional abandonment creates another type of threat to the character psychologically, training the character to reject themselves with messages like, "It's not okay to show feelings, or have needs, or make mistakes." Betrayal is not limited to people, however. Groups, systems, institutions, beliefs, even a trusted ideal can break faith or prove demoralizingly false.

Outsider — Perhaps the character believes the group they're ostracized from will give them a sense of personal identity or they harbor an unrequited love for someone who symbolizes belonging. Or maybe the character embraces their loner status out of a misguided belief they're protecting others from their problems. What matters is that the "group"—whether it's comprised of one or hundreds—represents the fulfillment of the character's deepest need. Lacking the support of a personal community system such as family or trusted friends puts the character at a disadvantage. For them "safety in numbers" is not an option. They don't have anyone to watch their back, and this creates apprehension in the reader. However, this rooting interest has to be supported by other traits, because sometimes there are healthy reasons for excluding someone from a group, such as violent or criminal tendencies.

Embarrassed or Humiliated — Embarrassment occurs when a character makes an honest mistake that's publicly exposed. Humiliation, on the other hand, occurs when someone deliberately makes the character feel bad about themselves in front of others. Will the character crumple under the emotional stress, retain his cool, or come out swinging? If it happens to a good guy, the reader will root for them to soldier on with dignity, and feel tension over the character's inescapable internal conflict. If it happens to the bad guy, the reader may enjoy a good laugh at the villain's expense while tensely anticipating payback lurking around the corner for other characters involved.

Hunted or Trapped — This trait carries the threat of higher stakes, usually injury or physical jeopardy of some kind. If some innocent person is also going to suffer should the character be caught, so much the better. If the target character is unaware someone is tracking them down or preparing a trap, then the reader's tension relies upon superior knowledge of the stalking character's plans. But if the target character is cognizant of the peril, then the internal conflict swirling around his personal stakes is highlighted. As the character is compelled to flight or fight, the reader roots for the character's escape and feels every inch of the noose tightening. Of course, it works in reverse if the character is the bad guy. Then the reader roots for them to be captured and feels tension whenever a chance arises for escape.

Unfortunate Accident or Natural Disaster — Be sure the bad things accidentally happening to the character serve as *complications to existing conflict* and not merely coincidences to pad a thin plot. If the reader knows a character is concealing their true nature (either good or bad) from others, this trait works very well to focus their anticipation on exposing the character's genuine self under pressure. Use judiciously and with extreme moderation, however, as random events usually lack either one or both of the two most essential ingredients of satisfying drama: intent and decision.

Chapter Seven

How the Character Treats Others

Instilling courage into a character builds the emotional bridge between the reader and the character. Tension traits keep the bridge maintained and in tip-top condition to support the flow of emotions between character and reader. But what guarantees the reader will actually enjoy spending time in the character's company?

The next category of rooting interests are Likability Traits, which focus on how the character treats other people, and evoke **affinity** in the reader. Ancient wisdom teaches, "Can two walk together, except they be agreed?" (Amos 3:3 KJV) Most people want to think of themselves as basically good, so if you want them to walk several hundred pages in the character's shoes, give the character virtues the reader can agree with.

Most readers experience Likability Traits with a sense of familiarity and equality. In *The Story Solution* Eric Edson says, "When a person finds your hero sympathetic, they...project themselves into your hero as their surrogate for the adventure ahead." (14) Whereas all three categories of rooting interests are designed to evoke *empathy* in readers, only Likability Traits are capable of generating *sympathy*. That means the reader understands, agrees with, and approves of the character's feelings, opinions, and behavior toward others. The character expressing these traits is neither admired nor pitied, but for the moment at least, exists on the same imagined moral plane as the reader.

Some classic examples of universally recognized virtues include:

Compassion

Consideration

Forgiveness

Generosity

Humility

Kindness

Loyalty

Responsibility

Thankfulness

Understanding

As universally recognized as these virtues are, the reader will remain stubbornly unconvinced the character possesses any of them if all a writer does is tell them, "Jane was kind and considerate." Virtues are portrayed not so much by the words on the page, as by the pictures those words create. Mental movies or video, if you will, of the character's spontaneous choices and actions. In other words, for the reader, seeing is believing. They must *see* Jane choose to be considerate of someone else, and *see* her act kind toward others. That's what Likability Traits are all about: *showing* instead of merely *telling* the reader that the character is someone worth rooting for.

The reader observes the character's behavior, and instinctively approves or disapproves of the consequences. Where Likability Traits are totally absent, the reader may feel edgy, offended, or even threatened by the character. Conversely, where Likability Traits are abundant, the reader feels safe, secure, and comfortable spending time with a character who will not violate but rather validates the reader's own sense of right and wrong. Because they feel free to agree with the character's choices and actions, the character in a sense becomes their avatar in the story. The reader is drawn into the story as if by magic as the character makes the same decisions readers like to believe they themselves would make, and takes the same actions they imagine they themselves would take.

Just because a character may demonstrate some or all of these virtues doesn't mean they're a saint or anywhere near perfect. No character worth a reader's respect wakes up one morning and blithely decides, "Today I'm going to be good!" Far from it.

These Likability Traits are born out of the fiery crucible of testing and internal conflict. Action only carries emotional weight and meaning in a story when it's the result of the character's intentional choice between two internal values, and thus demonstrates the resolution of an internal conflict. Characters are likable not because they are good, but because even when it's to their own hurt they struggle and fight the war within to be good.

Some genres, such as romance, require a healthy sprinkling of Likability Traits for its lead characters. Romance readers expect the hero and heroine to be genuinely good people who are likable enough to attract a mentally healthy life partner. Even the ever-popular kick-ass heroines or bad boy heroes are far from anti-heroes. Their rough and tough exterior is often a tool in the service of a strong moral code that includes loyalty to a higher cause and protecting the weak.

However, not all genres require likable lead characters or for lead characters to be likable all the time, and certainly there are successful protagonists who are not all that nice. Scarlett O'Hara, for example, willingly jettisons virtues such as truth, honor, and kindness in order to survive. However, while sympathy traits are never her strongest suit, Scarlett has an occasional humanizing moment.

Even the characters readers love to hate—villains—are stronger if they possess a few choice Likability Traits. This means more than giving them a cuddly puppy or a sick child to care about. To resonate as realistic, three-dimensional people, bad guys need to suffer internal conflict over their actions and choices. That internal conflict stems from their moral values. Yes, even bad guys have a virtue or two tucked away somewhere in the dark recesses of their soul. As their negative choices drag them on a downward character arc, they gradually abandon morality until they reach a place of real or metaphorical isolation at the end—a type of hell.

An example is the Evil Queen in season one of TV's fantasy series *Once Upon a Time*. On one hand, she hates Snow White for ruining her only chance at happiness. On the other hand, the person she loves the most is her father, who tries to comfort her lonely heart (a Likability Trait). Internal conflict develops when she tries to cast a terrible spell to ruin Snow White's happiness, but the only way to make the spell work means murdering her own beloved father. Her dedication to her goal is so great she sacrifices the moral value of devotion upon the altar of her hatred. It makes her a much more interesting character, and provides the audience an important opportunity to root *for* the villain: "No, don't do it! Choose a better way!" They're not rooting for her to succeed against Snow White, but rather rooting for her chance at redemption. The audience realizes she's digging her own pit deeper, isolating herself further from the love and happiness she craves.

The tragic irony fueling villains is they believe sacrificing whatever residual goodness they possess is justified, logical, perhaps even noble. In the Korean drama *City Hunter*, the primary villain believes his quest for revenge is a noble expression of loyalty to his best friend who gave his life for him. To the bad guy, murdering a bunch of corrupt power brokers is a just cause born out of unconditional love. He would feel like a bad person if he *didn't* take revenge.

That process of rationalization and self-justification for negative behavior begins with a Likability Trait, something that makes the antagonist feel morally secure about himself. However, pride always precedes a great fall. Villains focus too exclusively on how right they are to travel down a broad road to destruction, while protagonists focus and struggle to maintain their balance on the straight and narrow.

While even the most likable protagonist may and even should stumble or fall occasionally on his internal journey, part of climbing back onto their feet again and dusting themselves off involves embracing virtue and clinging fast to benchmark morality. That's why Likability Traits are multi-use. The protagonist doesn't just demonstrate a certain Likability Trait once and then forget about it. They return to it in fresh and original ways that keep readers emotionally connected to them while showing their maturing character arc.

WORKS FOR ANY CHARACTER

The following Likability Traits are so powerful that even one on the page can instinctively trigger an immediate feeling of affinity for a character. This is true regardless if the character involved is a nice-guy protagonist, an otherwise vile villain, or a walk-on character.

Guilt and Regret for the Pain His Mistake or Shortcoming Causes Others — If the character has hurt others in the past, this trait is essential to redeeming negative backstory. Readers will forgive a character for incredibly selfish, mean-spirited things done *in the past*—provided they're racked with guilt for it *in the present*. This proves to the reader the character's capacity for growth and self-awareness, even if the greater portion of their character arc lies ahead. If the character's moral mistake occurs in the present story, then the reader's sympathy hinges on how fast the character recognizes the suffering they inflicted on others and regrets causing pain. The longer it takes for this recognition of personal responsibility to occur, the more strained the reader's emotional connection to the character becomes. Instantaneous guilt, or as close to it as the character can get, yields the strongest rooting interest. This isn't about the character wallowing in self-condemnation. A line or two, at most a few paragraphs, are usually sufficient to get the point across while maintaining story momentum. Follow this simple three-part recipe: First, the character recognizes someone else's suffering; second, they acknowledge and own responsibility for causing pain; third, they experience genuine regret.

Relates Well with Animals, Children, and Elderly — *Animals:* Domestic animals with a history of companionship with humans have a sympathetic edge over wild or potentially dangerous animals, and small animals over large animals. The key to this rooting interest is properly setting up the animal as beloved, vulnerable, helpless, or in jeopardy. Establish the animal as someone's beloved or trusted pet, or in urgent need of the character's help. Even when hunting game for food, likable characters strive for mercifully clean kills and feel wretched if an animal is maimed or unnecessarily suffers. (An important exception to this trait involves dangerous animals who threaten the life of the character or others, then the rooting interest involved shifts from likability to tension as the readers focus on stopping the threat. An example is the drug dealer's attacking Rottweilers in the beginning of *The Dark Knight.*) *Children:* If children feel safe and happy around the character, readers accept it as a true indication of the person's heart and capacity for redemption. If the character's good with kids, especially those with special emotional, mental, or physical needs, all the better. Readers are eagerly willing to project themselves into a character who protects the weak and innocent. (A rare exception is if the child is neither innocent nor helpless, but a psychopath, then the rooting interest transforms from likability to tension.) *Elderly:* Readers find a character charming who patiently accepts the unique challenges of relating with the elderly. If the elderly person also happens to be as wise as their years are long, then their positive endorsement of the character can go far in convincing the reader they're someone worth rooting for.

Loves, Values, and Supports Worthy Family/Friends — If birds of a feather flock together, then a character is known by the company they keep. The virtues they admire and enjoy in others reveal a treasure trove about their own values. The reader takes stock of their friends, and automatically credits the character with sharing the same principals of right and wrong. Show them lending their emotional, social, or material support to kind, wise, or courageous people, and the reader will consider them kind, wise, or courageous. Readers also feel warm and safe in the presence of a character who knows how to love, free from selfish ambition or bitter jealousy. Where love exists, other virtues can take root and grow, as well. Love is the greatest and most powerful virtue of all because the other virtues only work by love. If a character truly knows how to express unconditional love toward someone, anyone, even a pet, then the reader knows the capacity exists within that person for every other worthy virtue, however unrealized at the beginning of their character arc.

Worthy Family/Friends Love, Value, and Support Them — This rooting interest can create affinity for even the most hardened or outright criminal characters. So long as the character has someone kind or wise in their life who loves or befriends them, the reader's willing to assume they must have some good in them no matter how deeply buried it may be beneath layers of emotional dysfunction. Award-winning romance author Mary Connealy says, "I had a really solid piece of advice from a contest judge once, who didn't like my heroine. She said, you make a character likable (brace yourself for the wisdom) by having other characters like them. Give them a friend, a pet, even the hero who is annoyed with the heroine, have them admit, on the page, that they like the difficult character, understand why she has the emotional shields, whatever. So, make your character likable by having other characters like them. Pretty simple, but it works."

Respects and Appreciates a Justified Rebuke — Being likable isn't about being perfect or never making mistakes. When the character inevitably steps out of line either in action or word, someone else is likely to suffer unfairly as a result. This is a very humanizing fault for a character to demonstrate, but can also be emotionally off-putting to readers who tend to disapprove of injustice. To redeem the character's mistake in the reader's perception, and win them huge bonus points in the likability department besides, have the target of the character's moral error rebuke them for their behavior. Identify the injustice to their face. The reader will be riveted to the page to find out how the character will respond—and like them all the better when they humbly acknowledge their fault, respect the person's dignity in standing up for themselves, and appreciate their courage and skill to cut them down to size.

WORKS FOR MOST CHARACTERS

The following Likability Traits are reliable stimulators of the reader's affinity for a character when they involve personal sacrifice. Anyone can afford to be nice if it costs them nothing, but when a character gives up something important it hooks the reader's heart.

Fights and Sacrifices for a Just Cause — The key, of course, is that the cause seems just not only to the character, but also to the reader. Which is why this rooting interest provides the writer with a great opportunity to explore meaty themes and the sometimes fine line between right and wrong, such as revenge versus justice. Sometimes the character not only fights for a just cause, but must fight to preserve the moral integrity of that cause from the corrosive influences of selfish ambition or bitter jealousy. This assures the reader the character truly understands what they're fighting for, and is not simply a hothead latched onto a convenient outlet for aggressive tendencies. The measure of what they risk sacrificing for the cause demonstrates the depth of their belief and commitment. Little risk, little conviction, little emotional response in the reader. Big (read: *personal*) risk, big conviction, big emotional response in the reader.

Risks or Sacrifices Life for Another — This trait puts everything on the line, the highest stakes possible, to redeem the life of someone else. "For the greatest love of all is a love that sacrifices all. And when a person sacrifices his life for his friends, this great love is demonstrated." (John 15:13 TPT) If it's paired with the Tension Trait of physical jeopardy, then this rooting interest packs a double emotional punch for the reader. Keep in mind life is comprised of more than the physical integrity of the flesh-and-blood body. Though a few people may be willing to risk their physical life to save someone else, even a stranger, from imminent death, how many are willing to risk a lifetime of unhappiness or pain so someone else can live a better life? The character may sacrifice some essential thing that makes life worth living, like freedom or love, without which their life will never be the same or whole again.

Egalitarian, Unprejudiced — Martin Luther King Jr.'s dream to be judged not by the color of his skin, but on the merit of his behavior and actions stirred the world. When a character similarly treats someone as their equal, especially those whom others ostracize or oppress based on natural differences, it stirs the reader's heart. The ability to relate unselfconsciously with others, regardless of skin color or social class or pedigree, easily makes the character stand out as someone the reader can feel comfortable around. Throw this trait into sharp relief by contrasting the character's egalitarian attitude with the prejudice or bigotry of their peers or authority figures. Make them risk disapproval in a tangible way, and readers will love them all the more.

Defends the Helpless or Victimized — This is an especially handy trait to use to establish rooting interests simultaneously for two different characters. On one hand, the reader will experience tension for the victim, while on the other hand they'll automatically feel affinity for the rescuer. The more instinctive and spur-of-the-moment the character's defense of the downtrodden, the more credible it will feel to the reader. What does the character risk? What do they sacrifice? Whether it's the business deal of the century, a parent's disapproval, or simply making the bus on time, make the character aware of what they're giving up. Make it personally important to them. Then make them instinctively throw it away because they can't stand by and do nothing or continue serving their own self-interest when someone is defenseless or in trouble. This trait is enhanced to a higher level if they jump to the defense of an abused/neglected child or animal.

Makes a Commitment and Keeps It, Even to Their Own   Hurt — The twin keys to this rooting interest are the moral value of their original commitment and the amount of pain it costs them later. The oath, duty, or responsibility they initially adopt is never unconsciously or accidentally acquired, but consciously accepted. Even if they can't imagine the full scope of what it means at the time, they know it means self-denial or hardship. But the commitment is a moral, rather than merely psychological one, meaning it involves more than their own wellbeing. Maybe it's a duty to God, country, or family. Maybe it's a duty to someone dead. Regardless, it's this responsibility to someone else's wellbeing that becomes their line drawn in the sand they will not cross no matter how dire the pressure or severe the personal loss or alluring the temptation. The other person involved becomes the personification or container of the moral stakes, and the reader gauges the character's true values and convictions by their resolution to stand in the gap to shield someone from harm.

WORKS FOR SOME CHARACTERS, BUT NOT OTHERS

The efficacy of the following Likability Traits depends heavily on the nature of the character and the specific circumstances involved in order to create affinity in the reader. If the character's motivation is altruistic and selfless, the reader responds positively, but if the character's motivation is manipulative, readers will despise them all the more intensely.

Encourages Others When They're Downcast — Who doesn't welcome people who bring with them hope to light the gloom of despair, confidence to drive back discouragement, or enthusiasm when energy flags? If the character goes out of their way to rally someone who's downcast, the reader can't help but warm up to them. Time is a precious gift, and if the character takes the time to give of themselves to mend someone else's bruised or broken spirit, they become an unselfish investor in that person's dreams. Every success that person experiences later on in the story will in the reader's heart be credited back to the character who found the right word to say, or held their hand, or gave them a shoulder to cry on, or a leg up the ladder. (Of course, the character must be sincere. The reader will feel irate if the character knowingly encourages someone in a foolish action that will cause harm.)

Generous, Caring, or Compassionate Act — A genuinely altruistic act, without expectation or guarantee of reward or personal benefit, makes a character very likable. Whether the recipient is a complete stranger, a bosom friend, or a beloved family member, makes little difference to readers. It's enough to know the character is a nice person willing go out of their way to lend a helping hand to someone in need. Of course, if the recipient is a thorn in the character's side or even an outright foe, then the character's act of goodwill is doubly generous and will stand out even more to the reader. Just beware of allowing the character to naively expect one good deed to inspire their enemy to turn a new leaf. Performing a good deed with the motivation of establishing an emotional or material debt on the part of the recipient is exactly the kind of manipulation that will turn readers off.

Lets Down Their Defenses in a Private Moment — It's tough being tough all the time, and in intimate moments when the character feels most safe and secure they're liable to let their emotional shield drop. This rooting interest works great teamed up with Tension Traits like betrayal or injustice, when someone takes unexpected advantage of the character's vulnerability to selfishly advance their own cause, and unfairly inflict pain. This rooting interest more commonly appears in Act Two, where the character's deepest core is painfully laid bare. Act One is generally too early to reveal the character's hidden fears, and they may be too busy barreling toward the conclusion in Act Three for these kinds of moments. But as they enter the new world of the middle and are compelled to adapt their attitudes and behaviors in order to advance their goals, the reader glimpses their true weaknesses and real fears. Whatever the genre—comedy, romance, suspense, thriller, etc.—every great story at its heart is a mystery, the puzzle pieces intimate issues of the heart. This rooting interest is a major clue to the solution.

Change of Heart — If pride goes before a fall, then humility and fairness pave the way for the character to be elevated in the heart of the reader. When a character swallows their pride by admitting they were wrong about someone or that an opponent is right about something, it shows the character's innate humility, honesty, and sense of fairness. This is especially effective if the character had very good reason to hold the other person in a bad light. Perhaps the other person wronged them or someone they loved. Perhaps the other person was caught in a compromising situation that casts doubt on their veracity or credibility. Then the character doesn't seem unreasonable to reject that person, at first. While swallowing their pride may be bitter for the character, it goes down sweet for the reader. Don't mistake this rooting interest for wishy-washiness or flip-flopping, though. Readers are annoyed by characters who either refuse to take a stand about anything (even if it's wrong) or who are carried hither and thither by every wind of opinion.

***Takes the Blame or Covers for Someone Else's Honest Mistake* —** The character voluntarily invites blame and punishment upon himself, which they don't deserve, for the sake of protecting someone else who's responsible. The key here is that they're not covering for a moral failure or crime, thus their action is noble instead of conspiring to harm. It was only a simple mistake, accident, or at worst misjudgment on the part of another. The character perceives the punishment may be harsher than deserved, or perhaps foresees longterm consequences best avoided. So the character jumps in and takes the blame because they believe, sometimes erroneously, that they're better equipped to handle the fallout than the guilty party. To successfully ignite the reader's rooting interest, this act needs to be motivated by mercy, not martyrdom, with no strings attached.

Chapter Eight

How the Character Treats Themselves

The third category of rooting interests encourages readers to look forward to the character's every appearance in the story and perk up with anticipation whenever they step onto the page. If tension builds the emotional bridge, and likability makes the journey enjoyable, then **admiration** enables readers to sink completely into that blissful oblivion called "suspension of disbelief" where they completely trust where the character is taking them.

What inspires someone to feel admiration? Let's trace this emotion back to its source.

We admire people who do certain things really well, who've accomplished mastery at a specific task. In other words, they are competent enough we can trust them completely in at least one particular area of life. In a story, that particular area of life should be central to the character's role in the plot and arc of internal growth.

Admiration Traits are derived from the character's psychological health. They are the products of how well the character has developed their own soul: their mind, their will, and their emotions. A flabby will and toneless emotions will never attain mastery in anything, and are nothing to admire in any character. But a soul rippling with self-discipline and honed by self-denial radiates the kind of irresistible power that compels admiration. Here is a force to be reckoned with, a character capable of making things happen.

Motion attracts attention, in nature as well as in fiction. Admiration Traits empower a character to be proactive instead of reactive in the story. It's absolutely essential that the protagonist be the most proactive character in the story, which means they drive the story and make it happen, especially at the key turning points. But even the most minor character earns their place in the story by making something happen that no other character could be responsible for. Reactive characters are pushed around by events like pawns on a chessboard, and will eventually bore readers, unless they find the inner fortitude to push back against the plot.

But just being very good at something isn't enough by itself to evoke a reader's admiration. If a skill comes too easily, falling on the character basically like ripe cherries from a tree, readers may feel jealousy, envy, or even disgust. At the very least, they'll feel bad about themselves because it suggests an inherent lack or inferiority in the reader that they couldn't have it that easily themselves. Think back to the girl in high school with the perfect metabolism who could eat like a horse and never gain a pound or pimple. Or the classmate in school who never cracked open a book or studied, and still got straight As. Objects of envy and jealousy? Yes. Admiration? Not so much, because the perfect complexion and the effortlessly perfect report card had little if anything to do with skill or competency.

The key to Admiration Traits is that they must make the reader feel inspired and empowered. This is accomplished by establishing how extremely hard the character has worked to attain and/or maintain proficiency at whatever they're good at. Practice makes perfect. Not rote repetition, but deliberate practice. Constantly stretching toward a goal just out of reach. Failing, failing, failing, then succeeding—only to move the goal a little farther and try again.

Often the character's training (no matter how unconventional) takes a lot longer than weeks or months, but rather *years*. Perhaps most of their life. Long before Malcolm Gladwell's controversial 10,000-hours-to-mastery theory, ancient wisdom asserted that practice makes perfect. Even if the character is a phenomenon or prodigy, it still takes years to season natural talent with the maturity that only comes by experience.

Acknowledging the hard work involved in honing specific skills is so essential to emotionally bonding characters with the reader that whole stories can be built successfully around the training phase alone. Examples from military stories include *An Officer and a Gentleman* and *Top Gun*. Many sports stories are also famous for this, such as *The Karate Kid, The Bad News Bears* and TV's *Friday Night Lights*.

Every character, regardless of genre or the type of story, rises in the reader's estimation when it's revealed how hard they've worked at something (even if the rest of their life is a mess). Point out the effort involved. All that's needed are a few brief lines of dialogue or action sprinkled here and there directing the reader's attention to the character's diligent efforts.

Why does hard work resonate so strongly with readers? It's about commitment, about making value choices requiring the character to sacrifice for mastery. They've made informed, intentional choices about where they spend their time and effort, and accept the consequences of neglecting other areas of life because they deem the trade-off worthwhile. We admire people who sacrifice in order to get good at something, even while we understand our own values may lead us to make different choices.

The drive for competency throws a dramatic spotlight on the character's internal motivations. Something of deep personal significance must be at stake emotionally to compel a person to embrace hardship and sacrifice when they otherwise don't have to. Especially if it's a skill that the majority of people in the world get along very well without or with only a mediocre knowledge of. But the unique dictates of this particular character's past, coupled with their personal values, made attaining a certain skill set essential to their sense of self-worth and inner wellbeing.

An example is Lee Yoon-sung in the international hit Korean drama *City Hunter*, whose entire life from childhood to adulthood is spent training to become a hardened warrior. Why? Because he yearns desperately for his emotionally-distant father's love, and is willing to work himself to the bone for the mere chance of earning his approval. Achieving mastery in combat means a lot more to him than merely the ability to knock down bad guys (though it does come in handy). It means living up to his parent's strict standards and eventually fulfilling his own destiny to avenge a terrible injustice.

In the long-running TV mystery series *Murder, She Wrote*, the protagonist is an English teacher who turned to writing bestselling mystery novels as a way to work through her grief after the death of her beloved husband. She uses her resulting skills of observation, objective reasoning, research, and psychology to solve real murders, but her attainment of mastery in her field was first driven by emotional needs.

In the TV inspirational drama *Touched By An Angel*, two experienced angels train a newbie to help people on earth find their way to the destiny God planned for them. While they rely on skills of patience and perception to accomplish their external goals, their internal motivation to hone those skills springs from their earnest desire to worship their Creator.

In other words, any skill the character masters is worth more than the sum of its parts. The emotional reward, above and beyond the material benefit, motivates the character's dedication.

Even outright villains benefit from Admiration Traits. The strength of a story is really found in the power of the opposition, because the harder the struggle, the bigger the protagonist's ultimate victory. Therefore, the villain needs to be very good at the skills they employ to accomplish their villainy. Those skills make the villain dangerous to the protagonist and any other beloved characters who get in their way, but the hard work to attain those skills also underscores their commitment to their cause. Readers respect dedication, and when sacrifices demonstrate a character will not be swayed from a goal even at great personal cost, the reader anxiously anticipates the sparks that will erupt when those purposes—backed up by the skills to attain them—come into conflict with someone else's.

WORKS FOR ANY CHARACTER

The following Admiration Traits are so powerful that even one appearance on the page can inspire the reader to delight in that character and trust they will take the story in a dynamic direction. This is true regardless if the character involved in a likable protagonist, an evil villain, or a minor supporting character.

Courageous and Persistent — This is the kind of spunk and mental/physical bravery that keeps a character from giving up, caving in, or quitting when the going gets rough. It is the one essential Admiration Trait every protagonist must have, because it keeps the character moving forward in the story. If the character is acting out of fear, they're moving away from the central conflict and kicking the story into reverse. So even if the character feels terrified, have them demonstrate courage by doing what they need to do in spite of the fear. An example is Joan Wilder in *Romancing the Stone*. She wasn't skilled enough to rescue her sister from Columbian drug lords, and she knew it, but even though she was afraid she did it anyway. That's courage. Even the fear of death (at least for themselves) can't stop or paralyze the character from taking motivated action. Note that this is not the same as foolishness, recklessness, or a death-wish— all behaviors which tend to unnecessarily place others in jeopardy. If the story goal is properly set up as described in Chapter Three, then this trait is automatically built into the protagonist. But it's listed here as a reminder to show it in specific actions throughout the story to keep the reader bonded to the character. The effectiveness of this trait is increased when combined with injury, injustice, or mistreatment, so the character has to push past pain or unfairness to keep going.

Perceptive — This trait goes beyond mere observation skills. The character is genuinely, unaffectedly interested in understanding people, how they think, and what they're going through emotionally. The character possesses the unique ability to instantly focus intense concentration on someone as though they were the only individual on the planet. While not a literal mind reader, their keen comprehension of another's emotional state sometimes makes it seem as though they can see through the other person's skin and decipher their thoughts. Because of this ability, the character is quick to spot even the slimmest indicators to what others are truly feeling—and the all-important motivational *why* behind their behavior. This skill requires instinct and sensitivity, and the character is only able to accomplish it because they're not so selfishly wrapped up in themselves that they're oblivious to what others are experiencing. This is a particularly desirable trait for protagonists in mysteries and heroes in romances.

Skilled, Hard Worker — Whatever skill the character has that's *central to the story*, they're the best there is at it. It may or may not involve their profession, but it definitely involves their occupation, what they spend their time working to be good at. The playboy protagonist in the romantic drama *An Affair to Remember* never held a job in his life, but he's world-famous as a skilled ladies' man and turns out to be a pretty competent artist, too. Readers will forgive a lot, but never lack of effort. If the character's a warrior, they've trained and practiced until they're the best. If they're a horseman, they're an expert judge of horseflesh and a superb rider. Even the popular non-conformist "slacker heroes" of modern times are skilled at something, even if it's only applying exceptional ingenuity at avoiding work. To locate a character's area of expertise, simply follow their passion and note where they've invested their attention and the resources available to them.

Wise and Powerful — Faint heart never won the day or the reader's heart, either, for that matter. Charismatic characters radiate power and leadership. They unselfconsciously step forward to take the point position to accomplish what needs to be done, and don't waste a lot of time arguing with nay-sayers or pretenders. They are the kind of person whom others trust unconditionally and instinctively turn to without question in time of stress or fear. When no one else knows what to do, this character has the bold, clever answers people need. They are the go-to person to get the job done when no one else can. People fight over who gets to have them on their side or team, because their help is deemed essential to success, and it feels like a death blow should their assistance be denied or withheld.

Protective — The more the character cares for someone, the more they want to protect them. They will marshall every ounce of strength and resource at their command. Nothing is held in reserve or off-limits from their total commitment to securing the safety of their loved one. While not suicidal about it, they hold their own life as a secondary concern, another resource to spend if required to guarantee their ultimate noble purpose. They're willing to set the whole world on fire if necessary to protect the ones they care about from danger. Gratitude is not required or expected. The object of their protective instincts may even be completely oblivious to the danger or the character's unheralded guardianship. It makes no difference to the character's commitment, which is unconditional. The key to this Admiration Trait is establishing the character has a reason that's vitally important to them to care about someone this much. The reader doesn't necessarily need for that reason to be spelled out right away, though. They just need to know there is one, and that it means more than life itself to the character.

WORKS FOR MOST CHARACTERS

The following Admiration Traits are reliable stimulators of the reader's trust in the character when they are coupled with the sense of responsibility to use their power and take corresponding action. Voting "present" doesn't cut it with readers. The character must apply their skill for a purpose.

Sees the Big Picture — This is the signature trait of all great masterminds. The character is unusually gifted with the ability to see the bigger picture. They're expert at connecting all the dots and following trails unseen by others. Puzzles of all kinds hold special appeal for them, whether it's a global conspiracy or the personal labyrinth of a human heart or a simple crossword puzzle. Their keen foresight allows them to prepare for the future, either financially or materially. Uniquely capable of planing at least a couple steps ahead of anyone else also equips them to be a master of manipulation. But because they comprehend longterm consequences better than most others around them, they also are burdened by a heavier responsibility for the ramification of their own actions. "I didn't mean for it to happen this way," is not going to be a credible excuse. Of course, the character still has to put their skill into action. Knowing what they should do but not doing it is a sin that will sorely try the reader's patience and which they are unlikely to easily forgive.

Patient and Self-Controlled — The character calmly accepts problems that arise to threaten their plans or personal suffering that tests their resilience and commitment. Those things might briefly annoy them, but trouble doesn't render them ineffectual by making them anxious or lose their cool. The character keeps their head at all times, remaining firmly composed even in the most stressful situations. The source of this admirable self-control is their unshakable conviction that giving place to anxiety guarantees a negative outcome, while patience and a good attitude is the only certain path to a perfectly desirable outcome. Patience is that indefatigable perseverance and singleminded focus that stays on course when others are running around like headless chickens. Don't let it deteriorate into passive-aggressiveness, though, or the story will stall. Then the reader may translate the character's apparent inactivity as stubbornness or a manipulation tactic and resent him for it.

Confident — It ain't bragging, it's just facts when the character shows full trust in their hard-earned, genuine abilities. The key to this rooting interest is that the character recognizes their own limitations. They're confident but never arrogant, therefore they're never caught overextending themselves and falling flat on their face due to pride. Authentic confidence leaves room to candidly admit with dignity what you *can't* do as well as what you *can*. When a character who honestly knows their own measure says, "This is bigger than I can handle," the reader can't help but go, *Oh, no!* because they trust that a confident character won't shirk and knows what they're talking about. Likewise, when the same character says, "Don't worry. I've got this," the reader watches expectantly for what they're going to do, trusting it's going to be something good. Eventually, the character must back up their self-assurance with real action. Otherwise, the reader is liable to feel the character just has an inflated or unrealistic opinion of themselves at best, and at worst is an outright liar.

Values Honesty — This rooting interest helps connect the reader with the character's inherent sense of fair play. Ironically, it does not mean the character never lies to themselves or others. They may even be a master at deception, or be involved in a profession or purpose that requires they live a lie, such as the protagonists in espionage or thrillers. Perhaps because they feel honesty is rare in their world, they value it even more highly when they do find it in others. They respect it as a sign of courage. That's why they themselves are always unflinchingly honest about the kind of person they are at heart and their self-interests in a situation; it's like they're giving others fair warning. They detest frauds who feign values like compassion or justice in order to emotionally or physically exploit the vulnerable or innocent. They also hate sarcasm, that impostor of truly clever wit, as a bully's disguise concealing the angry insecurity of cowards. Anyone they truly, deeply respect and care about can rest assured the character will never lie to them—although the character may not feel obligated to volunteer the whole truth, either. Honesty should always represent risk in a story, either tangible or personal. If there's nothing to win or lose by being honest, then there's nothing at stake and no purpose to it, therefore no emotional engagement for the reader.

Latent Sense of Justice — This is an essential trait of noble vigilantes like Batman and the City Hunter. The character never advertises it to others, but they possess a strong sense of justice that remains mostly hidden until circumstances occur that are suitable for its manifestation. They may even feign a careless or callous attitude in front of others if someone attempts to compel them to get involved and impress upon them their responsibility to stand up against oppression. They will not be forced into anything. But as soon as no one's looking, they go into action. If time is short, the character may have no choice other than to intervene publicly to prevent further injustice, but they'll escape attention as soon as possible. The idea of exploiting victims for personal aggrandizement by making a big show of rescuing someone is abhorrent to them. This rooting interest can be played as brief moments when the character steps in to remedy a witnessed injustice involving a passing stranger or walk-on character. Or it can be a slow-burn, developing over a long period of the story into a major set piece. However, if the character just watches with impotent, self-righteous disapproval from afar while someone suffers, and never takes action to stop the injustice, then readers will despise them as a hypocrite.

WORKS FOR SOME CHARACTERS, BUT NOT OTHERS

The effectiveness of the following Admiration Traits depends on the nature of the character and the specific circumstances involved in order to engender admiration for them. If the character uses their skills for good, readers will place trust in them, but if the character uses their abilities selfishly or to harm others, they'll be scorned.

Man or Woman of Mystery — The character is a keeper of secrets, both their own and others. This is partly because others know they can trust them, but also it's because they understand that knowledge is power. It's best managed wisely and frugally, because once spent, a secret can never be redeemed. This wraps the character is an unmistakable aura of mystery, and there are few traits as irresistible to readers as a walking enigma begging to be solved. What does the character know? When did they know it? How did they find it out? What are they going to do about it? All these questions and more rivet the reader's attention to the character. The more skillfully the character wields their secret knowledge for good, the more the reader's admiration grows. But should they ever use it for selfish, treacherous, or ignoble purposes, the reader will turn on them and root for them to fail.

Cultured Appreciation for Life's Finer Things — Regardless of the character's class or station, their life experiences have educated them to appreciate the value of the finer things in life. They may have benefitted from the best education money can buy, or enjoyed an unconventional upbringing and is largely self-taught. Either way, they recognize and practice good manners. The key to this rooting interest is that they're not a snob about it. While they prefer nice things because nice things are pleasant and enjoyable, they can be just as relaxed in a palace or a hut. The warmth of the summer sun on their face is to them every bit if not greater a treasure in life as gazing upon an old masterpiece in the Louvre. They may possess material luxuries, but luxury doesn't possess them. They're never greedy or driven by obsession for things (which would turn readers off in an instant), because they understand that all such enjoyment is fleeting and subject to rust or corruption or theft.

Cautious About Emotional Attachments — Emotional attachments are areas where the character is most vulnerable and personal stakes abound. Therefore they're super careful about whom they allow into their life and care for. Anyone they love could be used as leverage against them, and even become a target of suffering, injury, or death. That's why they don't wear their heart on their sleeve, or easily succumb to codependent relationships. This rooting interest is different than being cold or emotionally unavailable, which would feel as distancing to the reader as to another character. It's precisely because the character is capable of deep feeling that they guard their heart so well. That's also why if someone they allow deep into their life should ever betray them, the devastation would be unlimited.

Attractive — This rooting interest is often an essential trait in romances and most suspense thrillers, where physical attractiveness and/or athleticism are a recognized and legitimate clue identifying the lead character(s). But aside from genuine good looks, a person can be attractive in many other ways. They may have a glamorous and exciting profession that involves a lot of skill or danger or celebrity. If they're an eccentric, their non-conformist status as a rebel can also be daringly appealing, provided they pull it off with style and a dash of flair. Any unique way of living the character has voluntarily and successfully carved out for themselves will evoke admiration in readers. The key to showing that it's worked for the character is to surround them with other characters who admire them for it. Of course, there's not a lot to admire if they're insufferably vain about their good-looks, glamor, or fame. Even natural gifts should be maintained responsibly through hard work, and never taken for granted or lorded over others.

Sense of Humor — A healthy sense of humor, especially the ability to laugh at oneself, is always a popular trait. Comedians make careers out of it, but a character doesn't have to be a professional standup comic to win over readers. They admire characters who can marshall a quick, clever wit to diffuse tense situations or expose pretentious posturing and hidden agendas. The ability to engage unselfconsciously in child-like play with innocence and genuine enthusiasm is also incredibly winning. Readers can't help but admire glimpses of an unspoiled nature within a character. So long as their sense of humor is never intentionally hurtful, abusive, or bullying, any character capable of seeing the lighter side of life will have readers rooting for them.

Chapter Nine

Creating Complex Emotional Responses

"Laugh, and the world laughs with you; Weep, and you weep alone." — Ella Wheeler Wilcox, *Solitude, st. 1*

Although a character's feelings influence readers' emotions, they are not the same thing. Just because a character feels something intensely or experiences a range of emotions, doesn't automatically mean readers share the same response.

Yet empathy traits by themselves only evoke a limited number of reader emotions. To feel fully satisfied, readers need to savor a smorgasbord of complex emotional dishes.

If rooting interests are like spices, then the character's emotions are the food they season to taste for the reader's eager consumption. Without rooting interests attached to the character's feelings, they can weep buckets of tears or laugh themselves silly on the page and readers won't feel a thing. All the character's emoting falls flat. It's melodrama, and the only thing it inspires readers to feel is the uncomfortable sensation they're being manipulated.

Likewise, spices alone don't work as a main course. No one relishes gobbling down a bowl full of chili powder. Rooting interests ignite readers' emotional passion for the characters and the story, but those empathy traits must be connected to something dramatically substantive on the page or else the reader's response will quickly burn out. Characters shouldn't go through a story like automatons, coldly efficient at the tasks presented to them by the plot but emotionally unmoved. It makes for a very empty and frustrating experience for readers.

The character's emotions are the meat and potatoes of any story. Their emotional responses to other characters and events provide forward momentum to the plot and thematic resonance to the story.

If readers are first given a rooting interest in the character, that taste of tension or likability or admiration makes them want to dig in deeper. They'll look for clues to what the character's feeling, and share to some degree the character's emotions. That's when the reader's feelings and the character's feelings connect, creating a richly layered emotional experience. Now the reader is feeling tension, affinity, and/or admiration, *plus* joy, anger, love, jealousy, etc.

Let's examine how this works in the famous china-smashing scene from Margaret Mitchell's Pulitzer Prize-winning epic *Gone With the Wind*, where young Scarlett O'Hara confesses her love to Ashley Wilkes at the barbecue and is humiliated in front of Rhett Butler. The scene plays out much the same way both in the book and movie, so either version can be used as reference.

First, the scene is designed at the foundational level to capture readers' empathy. Scarlett's purpose is clear: she wants Ashley to marry her. Her plan to accomplish this is simple: tell him she loves him. What she has to lose is intensely personal: her future happiness, since she's convinced she can't love any other man, and is equally convinced he's in love with her.

Next, Scarlett doesn't sit on her hands waiting for something to happen. She makes it happen. For the sake of her future happiness, she takes forward action. She attempts something prohibited by every social rule she's been born and bred to. While decent young ladies are suppose to be getting an afternoon beauty nap, she sneaks into the library to ambush Ashley and blurts out her declaration of love. She's impetuous and her immaturity is stellar, but she's got that essential ingredient of every indisputably successful character: courage.

Those basic ingredients enable readers and the audience to savor the primal rooting interests spicing the scene. Below are the primary empathy traits manifest in the scene. The names of the characters they directly apply to most are formatted in bold.

Tension Traits

Secrets — This Tension Trait opens the scene, as **Scarlett** prepares to reveal the secret she's in love with Ashley.

Unrequited Love — Although there is little true tenderness in **Scarlett's** love for Ashley, it is a driving passion that rages like a consuming fire through her life.

Weakness or Vulnerability — **Scarlett** isn't often vulnerable, but there is a moment in this scene, however brief, where she abandons manipulative games and wears her heart on her sleeve.

Repressed Emotional Pain — **Ashley** is awash with repressed longing, sadness, and self-hatred. Late in the scene **Scarlett** tries to cover her own hurt and mortification with rage.

Loss — **Scarlett** loses Ashley when she humiliates herself in front of him with her confession of love and he rejects her.

Tells the Truth, but isn't Believed — **Ashley** explains he and Melanie are going to marry, that he doesn't want Scarlett, but she still refuses to believe he doesn't love her.

Blackmailed, Pressured, and Conspired Against — Scarlett tries to pressure **Ashley** into marrying her by unjustly claiming he led her on.

Outsider — **Rhett** only took sanctuary in the library because of his status as an outcast among the other guests.

Hunted or Trapped — From the moment Ashley closed the library door on Scarlett and himself, **Rhett** was trapped into witnessing the whole debacle.

Embarrassed or Humiliated — **Scarlett's** vanity is dealt a painful blow when Ashley rejects her, and then Rhett rises from the sofa to reveal her humiliation was witnessed by a notorious rake.

Likability Traits

Guilt and Regret for Mistake — **Ashley** regrets not making his previous commitment to Melanie clear to Scarlett from the start.

Lets Down Defenses in a Private Moment — After Ashley leaves her, **Scarlett** explodes and hurls a piece of china at the mantelpiece.

Respects and Appreciates a Justified Rebuke — When Scarlett furiously accuses **Rhett** of being no gentleman, he accepts it without offense as an appropriate and suitable observation.

Admiration Traits

Courageous and Persistent — **Scarlett** doggedly persists after Ashley to admit he loves her. She doesn't give up easily.

Confident — **Scarlett** takes this trait to the point of complacency. Nothing can shake her self-assurance in her own desirability to men.

Patient and Self-Controlled — **Ashley** patiently attempts to explain the mature reality of the situation to Scarlett.

Perceptive — **Rhett** sensed when his presence in the back yard was unwelcome, and removed himself. He also sizes up Scarlett in an instant.

Values Honesty — **Rhett** is forthright about his own nature, and, although Scarlett doesn't appreciate it in the slightest, bluntly honest about hers. ("And, you, Miss, are no lady...")

Sense of Humor — **Rhett** pokes fun at Scarlett's histrionics and laughs at her passionate defense of a man she swore moments before to hate all her life.

As well as being the central protagonist of the story, Scarlett is the driving force behind this particular scene, as well. So it's natural for her to possess the greatest number of rooting interests. She's the character it's most important for the readers and audience to bond with.

It's also the first scene where Rhett Butler has a speaking part and takes on real dynamic dimension as a character with his own unique attitude and values. Earlier at the barbecue, Scarlett glimpsed him from across a room when his bold glance gave her shivers, and she pried an earful of gossip about him from an acquaintance. But in this scene he becomes more than merely a handsome stranger with a bold gaze and a scandalous reputation. Contrasted against Ashley's laborious struggle to stand up to Scarlett, Rhett establishes himself immediately as her equal in every way.

Now let's dig into the meat and potatoes of the scene: the characters' emotions. These are the intangible energies within the character that provide momentum to their actions and decisions, thus driving and shaping the story. While readers and the audience are feeling various intensities of tension, affinity, and admiration for the characters, Scarlett is feeling:

Caution — as she peers over the bannister.

Hope — when she hears Ashley's voice in the front driveway.

Anxiety — fearing discovery as she slips downstairs.

Depression — from the environment in the library (she dislikes books).

Excitement — as Ashley approaches the library.

Yearning — as she indulges romantic fantasies.

Nervousness — as she gabbles broken prayers.

Confusion — when Ashley unexpectedly spots her.

Excitement and tension — when she draws Ashley into the library.

Happiness and pride — when she blurts out her confession of love.

Uneasiness — at Ashley's silence in the wake of her confession.

Alarm — when he casually dismisses her declaration.

Urgency — to make him take her seriously.

Passion — while insisting her undying adoration of him.

Fear — when he admits dully he cares.

Shock — when Ashley asserts his engagement to Melanie.

Denial — as she clings to what she knows, that he cares for her and she loves him.

Rage — when she accuses him of being a cad and coward.

Fresh anger, hurt pride and vanity, regret and scorching shame — a torrent of emotions as she inwardly acknowledges that he never did anything to encourage her throwing herself at him.

Desolation — in the wake of slapping him.

Overwhelmed — after Ashley leaves and the enormity of her actions sink in.

Self-hatred — for humiliating herself.

Fear — of everyone laughing at her as contemptuously as she treated others.

Startled and frightened — when Rhett first speaks up from the sofa.

Desperate dignity — when she challenges Rhett for not revealing himself sooner.

Anger — at his rudeness.

Fury — at his witnessing her humiliation.

Rage — when she defends Ashley to Rhett.

Violence and dignity — when she bangs the door behind her haughty retreat.

Ashley, the primary opponent in the scene, goes through a shorter range of emotions. Nevertheless, his feelings contrast dramatically against Scarlett's throughout the scene. At no point do the two characters come into emotional unity or share the exact same feeling about the same thing, which keeps the scene alive, unpredictable, and intensely interesting. Ashley feels:

Curiosity — when he unexpectedly comes upon Scarlett waiting inside the library.

Puzzlement and interest — when he allows Scarlett to draw him inside the room.

Consternation and incredulity — when Scarlett confesses her love to him.

Regret and pity — for how he must respond.

Misery — when he realizes she won't be easily put off.

Tenderness, pity, and self-hatred — when announcing his engagement to Melanie.

Shock and hurt — when she insults him as a cad and coward.

Misery and agony — when she rages at him and slaps him.

Both Scarlett's and Ashley's emotions fluctuate and change significantly from the beginning to the end of the scene. Scarlett begins the scene full of excitement and ends in a rage of dashed hopes and humiliation. Ashley begins the scene with curiosity and ends feeling miserable. In-between are fascinating textures of shifting emotions that give the scene depth and movement.

Because readers and the audience are first emotionally bonded to Scarlett via the specific empathy traits listed earlier, they are invested in caring how she feels. The reader experiences tension about the revelation of her secret to Ashley, so they are able to connect with Scarlett's feelings of hope and excitement. They admire her courage and persistence, so they can connect with her fear and desperation when Ashley rebuffs her. And because they understand how it feels to be caught when one's defenses are down, they sympathize with her anger and acute embarrassment in front of Rhett.

That's how the readers' primal emotional responses of tension, affinity, and admiration become layered with the character's complex emotional responses. The result is a richly-textured story that resonates in readers' hearts long after the last page.

Practice connecting readers with your characters' emotions by choosing a scene from your story. Make a list or use different colored highlighters to analyze which rooting interests are present in the scene. Does the protagonist or principal point-of-view character possess the greatest amount of empathy traits? Remember to give the antagonist or opponent in the scene some rooting interests, too. Even supporting characters benefit from having a few.

Next, create a separate list or use a highlighter to trace the main characters' emotions. What do they feel at any given time in the scene? Take them through a dynamic range of emotions, so they end the scene feeling differently about their goal, motivation, and/or conflict than how they began. Make their emotional responses visceral and alive through deep point-of-view techniques. Use metaphors and draw on the setting to help "show, don't tell" what the character is feeling.

FURTHER READING

Suggestions to deepen your understanding of how to "show, don't tell" character emotions:

Jill Elizabeth Nelson's *Rivet Your Readers with Deep Point of View,* "Chapter Four: Name That Feeling—Not!" Available in Kindle edition on Amazon and in print wherever books are sold.

Cheryl St. John's *Writing with Emotion, Tension, & Conflict,* "Part Two: Once More With Feeling." Available in Kindle edition on Amazon and in print wherever books are sold.

– Chapter Ten –
Putting Traits Together

The three categories of rooting interests detailed in the preceding chapters are similar to ingredients used in cooking. They infuse characters with unique flavors that give readers a sharp emotional kick. Truly standout characters satisfy the reader's hunger for specific emotional experiences. So what does your character taste like to the reader—salty, sweet, or spicy?

While the most gratifying flavors are layered and complex, never one-note, that doesn't mean that a muddying mix of traits will guarantee the finest outcome. Instead, give a character enough surplus traits from a single category to make them stand out, then fold in a healthy sprinkling of complementary or supporting rooting interests from the remaining two groups. This assures the reader will know what to expect emotionally when they metaphorically bite into the character, yet leaves them plenty to chew on as the story progresses.

What kind of emotional experience is the reader anticipating? A lot depends upon genre and the kind of story. Fans of suspense expect to feel tension, so suspense stories typically have protagonists loaded with Tension Traits. Thrillers, on the other hand, deliver larger-than-life thrills via protagonists abounding in Admiration Traits. Romances, regardless of sub-genre, often have heroes rich in Admiration Traits and heroines swimming in Tension Traits. Lighter stories are more likely to emphasize Likability Traits for their protagonists, while darker stories tend to dig deep into Tension Traits.

Genre considerations are important to understanding how to satisfy readers, but are only starting points. Many successful stories fly in the face of such generalizations, while cleverly fulfilling the reader's emotional expectations. Take, for example, the rule of thumb that heroes in romance novels should have loads of Admiration Traits. The reason is that most romance readers are women who read for the pleasure of vicariously falling in love with a man they can trust and feel safe with. Women want security. It's a primal need. So if a writer carefully selects a few choice Admiration Traits and emphasizes their importance in the story, she can pile on as many of the other categories' rooting interests as she wants.

An example is Patricia Veryan's *Time's Fool*, a historical romance set in the Georgian era. At first glance Veryan's story satisfies the convention of a hero rich in Admiration Traits. He's a returning war hero, the eldest son of a highly respected and wealthy family, who is also engaged to a Toast of society. These traits are vital to the plot, but Admiration Traits remain dominant for only the first scene before being overtaken and surpassed by another category of rooting interests.

Scandal has ruined his family's reputation so that the hero's name alone is enough to invite brutal beatings on the street by random strangers. Financial reverses have stripped his estranged family of everything, and they teeter on the edge of debtor's prison. And last, but certainly not least in a romance novel, his fiancee (who also happens to be the heroine and the great love of his life) falsely accuses him of being a gold digger and dumps him. Not to mention, he's also still recovering from wounds that nearly cost his life. Almost every resource he might naturally have possessed to secure his family and win his lady are promptly stripped away from him. He embarks upon the story as a true underdog pitted against the overwhelming prejudice of society as well as an elite and well-funded conspiracy to overthrow England. In short, Tension Traits reign supreme.

Another example is the incredibly likable hero in the Taiwanese romantic comedy *Love Myself or You?* (aka *Pleasantly Surprised*). The audience's genre-based emotional needs are met right away by a few select Admiration Traits. He's fair and just, confident without a shred of arrogance. He's sensitive to the heroine's emotions and genuinely invested in understanding her. And the hero's masterful skill as a French chef is an essential component of the plot. Where this hero really shines, however, is in his Likability Traits. He's got friends and family who love him, and whom he loves back unconditionally. He relates really well with kids. He's egalitarian and humble, even though he's the boss' son. He's an encourager. He's always doing something nice for others, without any strings. If he makes a mistake that causes someone pain or suffering, he feels terrible guilt and regret for it. And he's a genuinely warm, kind, caring person.

Next, examine the needs of the external plot and consider what kind of expectations a probable blurb might elicit in the reader. An example is the romantic comedy *While You Were Sleeping*. A possible description of the plot might read: *When a lonely transit worker's heroic rescue of a handsome stranger introduces her to his family at Christmas time, a misunderstanding lands her in the role of the comatose man's fiancee. Can she avoid hurting them and breaking her own heart when she falls in love with her unwitting groom's suspicious brother?* The plot requires the protagonist be likable enough to quickly win over a family of total strangers, but who is also a bit of an underdog. So the writers created Lucy with oodles of Likability Traits and a generous smattering of Tension Traits, along with a few choice Admiration Traits. The audience's expectations would have been sorely disappointed if the proportions were reversed, resulting in a mismatch between story and protagonist.

The character's internal journey also informs the choices a writer makes when equipping the character with rooting interests. Because of the moral and psychological condition the character begins the story with, some rooting interests are off-limits, at least until they grow into them. In *As Good As It Gets*, the protagonist really doesn't relate well at all with animals. He throws his neighbor's dog down the garbage chute in the first scene of the movie. Of course, later this rooting interest is redeemed when he winds up dog-sitting for the neighbor, which is a distinct sign of growth in his internal arc. Another example is the comedy *Liar, Liar,* where the character has the Admiration Trait of being really skilled at his job as a divorce lawyer. However, because his character arc involves going from falsehood to truth, initially he is necessarily devoid of another Admiration Trait—valuing honesty. That's a trait he must grow into as the story progresses.

The story's theme informs trait choices, as well. Certain thematic issues are organic to specific rooting interests. Tension Traits frequently focus on issues of hope and fear. Likability Traits often revolve around issues of love and shame. Admiration Traits are grounded in issues of faith/confidence and anger.

Take a moment to jot down your story's genre, and what kind of emotional experience readers are likely to anticipate. Are their expectations more likely to be met by a character with a majority of Tension Traits, Likability Traits, or Admiration Traits? If your story is an exception, pick a couple choice cardinal traits to highlight in order to satisfy the reader's genre expectations.

Keeping the main events of your external plot in mind, write down some traits the protagonist needs in order to credibly navigate the story. Does the plot require them to be an underdog, or really likable, or competent at something? These are clues to which traits to focus on.

Consider the protagonist's character arc. Which traits are necessarily absent at the beginning of their internal journey but which they grow into by the end? Write these down.

Finally, think about the story's theme. What are some of the issues involved in the character's major decisions? What is the lesson they learn at the end? Do the answers to these questions suggest an emphasis on the issues of hope/fear present in many Tension Traits? Love/shame issues found in Likability Traits? Or faith/anger issues manifested in Admiration Traits?

For practice, let's examine how the three categories of rooting interests are combined in one of the all-time classic underdogs of TV and film, Dr. Richard Kimble of *The Fugitive*. The genre is classic suspense, and the audience expects to feel a lot of tension from the man-on-the-run premise. The plot requires a lot of Tension Traits, but the character also needs a good supply of Admiration Traits just to survive. At the heart of the theme is a quest for truth that's energized by carefully selected Likability Traits.

Right away in the movie, this character is packed with rooting interests that evoke immediate tension in the audience:

- *He loses his wife.*
- *He's attacked and frantically struggles with her killer.*
- *He's not believed by the authorities when he tells the truth.*
- *He's falsely accused and convicted of her murder.*
- *He's in extreme physical jeopardy when the prison transport bus crashes.*
- *He's injured in a train wreck.*
- *The credit for the protagonist's heroic act of compassion toward an injured man is stolen by a cowardly prison guard.*

- *He's hunted down by federal marshals and trapped in a tunnel.*
- *He's in extreme physical jeopardy when he jumps into a raging river.*
- *He's haunted by grief for his late wife.*
- *A fugitive without means, he suffers financial hardship.*
- *He's trapped by police in a seedy basement apartment.*
- *He's chased by federal marshals through a federal building and narrowly escapes being shot and captured.*
- *He's betrayed by a trusted friend.*
- *A hit man attacks and tries to kill him on the El.*
- *He's injured apprehending the man behind his wife's murder.*

At first glance the above list may appear to be a sketch outline of the plot, but if so that's because these rooting interests are incorporated into the story as essential ingredients. They aren't dropped in at random. Every trait bonding the audience empathetically with the protagonist simultaneously serves to advance the story.

Next let's look at how the dominant rooting interest (tension) is supported by the addition of specific Likability Traits:

- *He was in love with his wife, and she loved him.* — This contributes personal stakes and motivation for his obsession to find her killer.
- *He risks his life to save an injured prison guard.* — This heroic act of compassion triggers the beginning of the opponent's (Deputy Gerard) reluctant character arc from cynicism to belief.
- *He relates well with kids and risks his freedom to save the life of a child.* — Proves to the audience that his ordeal hasn't calloused him, that he's still a compassionate protector of the weak and helpless. He's still true to himself and his calling.
- *He has friends who help him.* — Character witnesses are important, especially when the character is accused of a heinous act. It helps the

audience root for him if people who know him are rooting for him, too. Also, it helps advance the plot.

• *He exposes unethical and immoral behavior that's endangering people's lives.* — This Likability Trait highlights the story's climax, and satisfies the audience that the journey was about something greater than revenge for personal suffering. The whole story world is made safer because of the protagonist's moral code.

Now let's see how Admiration Traits are layered in:

• *He's a skilled and respected physician.* — This is actually why he was targeted by the villain, which is another way of making him the victim of unfairness.

• *He's attractive, good-looking and cultured.* — The villain's personal motivation for persecuting the protagonist: envy.

• *He's important to others.* — Other doctors rely on him to assist in difficult surgeries, which unwittingly upsets the hit man's plans. Otherwise, Kimble would be dead along with his wife and the story would be over before it began.

• *He makes a death-defying leap off a dam.* — Demonstrates his courage and persistence to pursue his goal.

• *The people in his life admire him.* — Provides motivation not only for his friends to help him, but for the villain to justifiably fear him and desperately try to stop him.

• *He's smart and clever.* — Traits recognized by others and demonstrated by his methodical investigation of the murder.

• *While wanted by the authorities, he bravely walks into a federal building to see a suspect.* — His daring thrusts him into a near-death confrontation with Deputy Gerard, but ultimately goes a long way toward turning his opponent into an ally.

- *He never gives up.* — Persistence that earns the grudging respect and admiration of Deputy Gerard.

The rooting interests roughly break down into the following proportions: 55% Tension Traits, 27% Admiration Traits, and 18% Likability Traits. Dr. Richard Kimble has twice as many Tension Traits as Admiration Traits, and three times as many Tension Traits as Likability Traits. While his character is designed to successfully engage the audience's emotions on all three levels of physical, moral, and psychological resonance, the emphasis on Tension Traits fulfills the audience's expectations for a suspense story.

If you know the details of your plot, take the time now to write out a simple step-outline similar to *The Fugitive* example above, focusing on your protagonist. If the story is still in the developmental stage, brainstorm some things that might happen. Group events/circumstances by their associated rooting interest category. Pay special attention to make each rooting interest trait essential to the story as a whole, not merely dropped in piecemeal. When finished, count how many traits are Tension Traits. How many are Likability Traits? Admiration Traits? If necessary, tweak until one category comprises at least fifty-percent of the total, so the character has a vividly discernible flavor.

Chapter Eleven

Using Empathy Breakers to Strengthen the Reader-Character Bond

Few successful stories have perfect characters who do no wrong. Flaws are integral to building a complex character with an internal journey who arrives at a thematically meaningful destination at the story's end. This is no less true for antagonists/villains than for protagonists.

All flaws are not created equal. They impact the emotional bond between reader and character differently. Understanding how to balance flaws with rooting interests is an important step in maintaining the reader's engagement with the story, and delivering the feelings they crave.

If the forty-five rooting interests examined in earlier chapters are turned on their head, they transform into forty-five flaws or "empathy breakers." Some of these can be readily used to enrich the character's internal journey. Others are actually a necessary part of making the reader experience closure and feel everyone received their just desserts. A few are perfect attributes for villains, as they shatter any chance the reader will root for that character's success.

TENSION turns into HORROR

These five Empathy Breakers work to mark any character as someone to root *against*. If the character is the protagonist, giving them one of these traits could be deadly to the reader continuing to care about them. If the character is the villain, these are great ways to guarantee the reader will fear and despise them. There's no excuse that can redeem or repair the emotional bond between readers and a character who...

• *Deliberately mistreats someone or perpetuates a gross injustice against someone they know to be innocent or vulnerable. Especially if they do it just because they can, to prove their power.*

• *Pries and snoops into others' private affairs. Compulsive tattle-tale who couldn't keep a confidence if their life depended on it. Blurts out secrets at the worst possible time for monetary gain, to appear important, or to watch someone suffer from its exposure.*

• *Constantly complains and whines about emotional wounds they've suffered, as though the world owes them.*

• *Exploits the weak or vulnerable for their own selfish interests.*

• *Coldly rejects a true and honest love for the sake of selfish ambition, without regard for the other person's emotional/physical suffering. The person could be their romantic lover, a platonic friend, or a devoted family member.*

The next five Empathy Breakers work to turn readers against most characters, so they work really well for villains. But a protagonist can get away with them, provided they have an overwhelmingly good reason, such as taking extreme action to stop a bad guy who's threatening others or to protect an innocent from greater harm.

• *Deliberately injuring, poisoning, or disabling someone so they cannot continue their present course of action.* (Can be redeemed if it's accidental, to stop a bad guy, or to protect an innocent person from greater harm, especially if the character assumes the victim's place in a sacrificial act.)

• *Placing someone in physical jeopardy. Especially if it's either through reckless-ness, cowardice, or cruelty.* (Can be redeemed if it's an unintentional mis-take and is genuinely regretted, or a deliberate attempt to stop a bad guy.)

• *Withhold companionship so as to make someone feel lonely and lost.* (Can be redeemed if it's a noble sacrifice the character makes to protect some-one from a worse fate. Especially if they themselves suffer loneliness and grief as a result.)

• *Refuses to believe someone when they're telling the truth.* (Can be redeemed if pivotal evidence is unjustly withheld from the character, so that any reasonable person would be compelled to disbelieve the truth-teller, too.)

• *Blackmail, pressure, or conspire against someone.* (Can be redeemed if done for a noble, unselfish, or patriotic cause to protect others.)

The last five Empathy Breakers from the Tension Traits category can turn readers against the character, or actually bond them closer. It all depends on whether the reader feels the victim deserves to be treated this way. It's a question of does the punishment fit the crime? If so, then the reader experiences it as justice. If not, *Boo! Hiss!* Nevertheless, if a character has other traits to counterbalance these pitfalls, they can still be redeemed as part of a story-length character arc.

• *Abandons and betrays someone who has the rightful expectation of loyalty and fidelity.* (Can feel justified if the person betrayed is a traitor to faith, family, country, etc.)

• *Ostracizes someone, treating them as an outsider or turning the community against them as an outcast.* (Can feel justified if the outcast is a danger to peace, person, or property.)

• *Embarrasses, humiliates, mocks, or ridicules someone.* (Can feel justified only if the put-down is directed toward negative choices or behaviors. Feels extremely alienating if it stems from bigotry against a character's race, gender, handicap, etc.)

• *Hunts down or traps someone.* (Can feel thrillingly justified if the targeted character is a predator of the innocent.)

• *Fate's whipping post, bounced passively around the plot by one unfortunate accident or natural disaster after the next.* (Can feel like karma or divine justice if it occurs at the denouement, but tricky to pull off satisfyingly without deteriorating into Deux ex machina. A successful example is James M. Cain's *The Postman Always Rings Twice.*)

LIKABILITY turns into REPULSION

These five Empathy Breakers work to mark any character as someone to root *against*. If the character is the protagonist, giving them one of these traits could be deadly to the reader continuing to care about them. If the character is the villain, these are great ways to guarantee the reader will detest and loathe them. There's no excuse that can redeem or repair the emotional bond between readers and a character who is...

• *Utterly indifferent to and uncaring of the pain their mistakes or shortcomings cause others.*

• *Treats animals, children, or the elderly with callousness, contempt, or outright cruelty. Especially if the animals are small, beloved pets, or the children are sweet and innocent, or the elderly are kind and vulnerable.* (Important exception: if it's an unbearably irritating animal who is not associated at the time as the object of anyone's affection, then the character's behavior may be briefly tolerated by the reader. An example is *As Good As It Gets*. Or if the animal is a dangerous threat, deadly force in the service of self-defense actually strengthens the reader-character bond. An example is the drug lord's Rottweilers in *The Dark Knight*.)

• *Enjoys, esteems and is loyal to family or friends who are unkind, cowardly, or cruel because they validate the character's own corrupt, mean-spirited values.*

• *Unkind, cowardly, or cruel people enjoy, esteem, and are loyal to the character because they recognize the character as a kindred worm-eaten spirit.*

• *Haughtily rebuffs a justified rebuke from one whom they've wronged, and bitterly hates any who dare stand up against their abuse.*

The next five Empathy Breakers work to turn readers against most characters, so they work really well for villains. But a protagonist can get away with them, provided they have an overwhelmingly good reason, such as debilitating personal phobias/handicaps or competing loyalty to a nobler, higher cause.

• *Strategically withholds their assistance from a just cause. Especially if it's at a critical hour of need, and they have the ability or resources to make the difference between victory or defeat.* (Can be redeemed if the character instinctively wants to help, but pre-existing or competing loyalties to faith, family, country, honor, etc., tie their hands.)

• *Puts someone else's life at risk or sacrifices others to save themselves.* (Can be redeemed if they're paralyzed by fear, broken psychologically, or tricked/compelled into it against their will, but even then only if they're haunted by regret and guilt. They still might have to make the ultimate sacrifice of their own life before the end.)

• *Snobbish, bigoted, or prejudiced.* (Can be redeemed if the offending character is depicted as a victim of their upbringing, and their character arc involves overcoming prejudice to eventually defend the oppressed.)

• *Oppresses the helpless or victimized.* (Can be redeemed if they're compelled to act against their own will and values, hating themselves for what they have to do in service to a larger, nobler cause. Examples include undercover cops and spies playing roles which demand they partake in abuse and corruption in order to bring down criminals or enemy states.)

• *Makes a commitment and then breaks it for selfish advantage.* (Can be redeemed if the character is forced to break their promise in order to protect someone in danger—in which case, it isn't selfish. Or, if they immediately regret the hurt their selfishness causes others, though the reader's trust in them will be sorely damaged.)

The last five Empathy Breakers from the Likability Traits category can turn readers against the character, or actually bond them closer. It all depends on whether the reader feels it's intended as "tough love" designed to challenge the other person to be stronger. If so, then the reader experiences it as selflessness and compassion. If not, they'll feel the character's just a big old meanie. Nevertheless, if a character has other traits to counterbalance these moral pitfalls, they can still be redeemed as part of a story-length character arc.

• *Criticizes, rebukes, or reprimands someone when they're already discouraged and downcast, making them feel worse for a perceived mistake or shortcoming.* (The reader can still care about the character if they're desperately trying to shock the person out of debilitating self-pity and aren't being cruel.)

• *Stingy, calloused, or selfish act.* (The reader can still care about the character if they're bravely establishing healthy barriers in a previously exploitative relationship, and suffers emotionally for being accused of selfishness.)

• *Erects impenetrable emotional barriers around their heart, even in private moments. Seems as though they care for no one. Especially if they're coldly unresponsive in the face of death or tragedy.* (The reader can still care about the character if they experience strong emotion inside but are so concerned about burdening others, they hide it.)

• *Unreasonable, rigidly opinionated, and too proud to change their mind even in the face of incontrovertible evidence.* (The reader can still care about the character provided it's a front they put on to deliberately challenge someone to work harder to prove themselves. Or if the character's assurance is energized by personal experience and concern others are being hoodwinked and jeopardized by a master manipulator.)

• *Blames someone else for their own foolish mistake or selfish behavior.* (The reader can still care about the character if they're trying to deflect attention from a weakness or vulnerability they fear will result in rejection and earnestly tries to do better or avoid the same mistake next time.)

ADMIRATION turns into SCORN

These five Empathy Breakers work to mark any character as someone to root *against*. If the character is the protagonist, giving them one of these traits could be deadly to the reader continuing to admire or trust them. If the character is the villain, these are great ways to guarantee the reader will angrily scorn them and abhor the degradation they inflict on others. There's no excuse that can redeem or repair the emotional bond between readers and a character who is…

• *Cowardly and irresolute. Draws back from the threat of pain or discomfort. Gives up, caves in, and quits at the first sign of pressure. Especially despicable if they leave others in the lurch.*

• *Callous, obtuse, or too focused on themselves to recognize others' feelings, social undercurrents, or power plays.*

• *Incompetent, lazy worker. Especially if their ineptitude places others at a dire disadvantage or in physical jeopardy.*

• *A fool or a weakling. Especially if they're unfortunately in a position of authority over better men.*

• *Neglects, exploits, or endangers those in their care. Especially if the person is someone the character has a natural obligation to watch out for, such as family, friends, or soldiers under their command.*

The next five Empathy Breakers work to turn readers against most characters, so they work really well for villains. But a protagonist can get away with them, provided they have an overwhelmingly good reason, such as extreme emotion short-circuiting their normally rational and clear-thinking mind. Terror for a loved one, burning guilt for a personal failure, or an obsession to avenge an innocent victim, are all understandable motivations for which the reader will extend grace.

• *Tunnel-visioned. Either they're so focused on their greatest fear they can't properly assess or take advantage of real opportunities for success, or they're so zeroed in on their goal that they rush ahead, oblivious to the collateral damage left in their wake.* (Can be redeemed if the character's fear or goal is directly connected to the health, safety, or welfare of a loved one in imminent jeopardy.)

• *Impatient, short-tempered, and loses control. Especially if the character loses their head in emergency situations and puts others in peril.* (Can be redeemed if the character has recently suffered a severe shock or personal loss, but they need to snap out of it before long.)

• *Barraged by self-doubt, trapped in uncertainty.* (Can be redeemed if it is triggered by a debilitating defeat, and only lasts for a short duration.)

• *Compulsive liar, who doesn't recognize when they're better off telling the truth because they consider honesty in himself or others a game for suckers.* (Can be redeemed if they're capable of feeling regret for the pain their dishonesty causes someone they love.)

• *Power monger or bully. Likes to swim with the sharks and imagines themselves the biggest shark in the ocean. The weak, helpless, or vulnerable are food for them, and they think it's the other person's own tough luck if they can't look out for themselves.* (Can be redeemed if there's someone disadvantaged in their life that they sincerely care for and strives to protect, especially if the character suffers abuse for standing in the gap.)

The last five Empathy Breakers from the Admiration Traits category can turn readers against the character, or actually bond them closer. It all depends on whether the reader feels that in spite of the flaw, there's still sufficient reason to trust the character. Is the character psychologically healthy enough to accurately assess their own behavior, but feels pressured by outside forces or extenuating circumstances to resort to bad behavior? If so, the reader will still accept them. But if they truly feel entitled to act out negatively, belligerently denying the inevitable consequences, then the reader will regard them with misgivings at best and cynicism at worst.

• *Makes others feel awkward and uncomfortable by consistently sharing too much information about themselves, especially private matters.* (The reader can still trust the character if the TMI is calculated to provoke a certain reaction, or if the character mistakenly assumed the other person was already intimately acquainted with the situation.)

• *Greed for riches and luxury, so the character sacrifices manners or dignity for them. Especially if they steal or rob from others.* (The reader can still trust the character if their motive is necessity rather than lust, such as they're forced to steal basic necessities for their own or others' survival, or only takes from the corrupt and not for personal gain, a la Robin Hood.)

• *Emotionally clingy. Wears their bleeding heart on their sleeve. Fantasizes overblown and obsessive emotional attachments for people who simply act nice or well-mannered.* (The reader can still trust the character if they respect the other person's privacy and personal boundaries, like a secret guardian, without crossing the line into stalker territory.)

• *Vain about their appearance or powers of attraction. Arrogantly assumes they are irresistible and God's gift to the opposite sex.* (The reader can still trust the character if their life experience gives them a rational reason for feeling this way, and when they're inevitably disabused of this notion, they accept the truth with humility instead of outrage or vindictiveness.)

• *Vicious sense of "humor" designed to tear people to bloody shreds, leaving them feeling inferior and horrible about themselves.* (The reader can still trust the character if their motive is selfless or noble, such as deliberately alienating someone to remove them from danger, and they bitterly regret the pain they inflict.)

Refer to the earlier chapter on "Quick and Simple Characterization" to determine the character's central flaw. A flaw is the erroneous behavior and/or belief that is the character's greatest hindrance to genuine success, but which they consider a necessary resource for survival. Review the above Empathy Breakers to select negative traits showing the character's flaw in action.

If the character is a villain, they will make a sharper emotional impression on the reader if they have at least one out the first five "unredeemable" traits in any Empathy Breaker category: Tension/Horror, Likability/Repulsion, or Admiration/Scorn. If the character is the protagonist, pay special attention to *avoid* the first five "unredeemable" traits from each category. Most stories' protagonists do very well drawing their flaws from the second and third sub-groups in each Empathy Breaker category.

While it is doable to start a protagonist on their journey with "unredeemable" negative flaws, it's a huge challenge to pull off successfully, requiring great skill and timing in revealing each and every trait to the audience. Often, readers may be unwilling to stick around for the ride. Therefore, other characters assume the lead role for awhile so the reader has someone to emotionally invest in.

An example is the Korean historical drama *Bridal Mask* (aka *Gaksital*). Imperial policeman Lee Kang To is the story's protagonist, but in the first quarter of the 28-episode series, he does everything he can to earn the epithet *bastard!* hurled at him by his fellow oppressed Koreans. Working for the Japanese in the 1930s during Korea's Dark Ages, he's a defiant traitor to his own people and shares in blatantly oppressing the poor and helpless to get ahead. He cruelly beats his mentally disabled brother, who loves him. He even betrays his first love, who's a Korean patriot, by torturing and shooting her.

Yet through it all, Kang To has a friend and a few family members who continue to care about him, hoping against hope along with the audience that he can change for the better. Nevertheless, the audience cannot root for him in his unredeemable state during the beginning of the series. So who can they emotionally attach to until Kang To pulls his act together and makes some progress on his internal journey to a healthier, moral protagonist worthy of the role?

The character who really charges the audience's emotional batteries is the mystery man behind the Bridal Mask, who appears out of nowhere to skillfully vanquish his countrymen's Japanese oppressors. No personal risk or sacrifice is too great in his courageous fight for justice. As the audience gains increasing insight into his real identity, they bond deeply with a man who loves children and his family unconditionally. A man who invites gross injustice upon himself in his quest to protect the genuinely weak and helpless. Bridal Mask is the character the audience embraces until Kang To lays aside his unredeemable empathy-breaking traits and matures into someone they can bond with.

When a character other than the protagonist carries the reader's rooting interest for a significant portion of the story, especially at the beginning, it's important that the supporting character's goal, motivation, and conflict entwine with the protagonist's. His fate must be intrinsically linked with the protagonist's internal journey, so that the character the reader is rooting for will succeed or fail because of the protagonist's willingness to change and grow. Thus the rooting interest character becomes a "stakes character," a personification of the protagonist's personal stakes in the story. This ensures the reader's attention continues to be drawn inexorably back to the protagonist, no matter how much readers may initially resist caring about them.

In *Bridal Mask* the title character's efforts to free the Korean people from oppression are ferociously resisted at every turn by Kang To, who mercilessly hunts him down. Because he is a skilled and courageous police detective, the audience feels the noose tightening around Bridal

Mask, whom they're rooting for, and hope against hope Kang To comes to himself before tragedy inevitably erupts.

It's worth noting that when the protagonist begins the story in a seemingly unredeemable place psychologically or even morally, they may need to suffer greatly for their sins before readers are willing to begin rooting for them. It's not that readers are sadistic, but their sense of justice needs to be satisfied before they're comfortable climbing onto the protagonist's bandwagon. In *Bridal Mask*, Kang To's unredeemable traits drive him headfirst into an emotional wall that breaks him heart and soul. He suffers extreme emotional trauma as a direct result of his empathy-breaking behavior. The audience is satisfied that the punishment fits his crimes, and even begin to feel sorry for him and worry that the intensity of his suffering may drive him mad. Thus develops the audience's emotional investment in a character they initially loved to hate.

Write down the Empathy Breaker traits selected for your character. If the character is the protagonist, pay careful attention that their positive bonding traits outweigh their negative flaw traits. Unlike rooting interests, treat these flaw traits like hot sauce in a favorite food dish. A little will go a long way. On the other hand, if the character is the villain, their negative flaw traits should outweigh their positive bonding traits, lest they threaten to steal away the reader's emotional investment in the protagonist.

If the Empathy Breaker traits are for the protagonist, describe how each trait will be redeemed in the heart of the reader and ultimately strengthen their emotional bond with the character. For example, in Georgette Heyer's historical romance *The Grand Sophy*, the hero has a notorious temper that frequently keeps his entire family on edge. But the reader extends grace to him because they are given to understand early on the unfair and intense pressure he's selflessly shouldering to save his spendthrift family from ruinous debts.

Chapter Twelve

Validating the Reader's Emotional Response

A vital component of building an emotional bond between the reader and the story involves developing the reader's trust in the writer. It doesn't matter whether it's the first book the reader's ever read by that author, or the tenth, or hundredth. The reader perceives instinctively within the first few scenes, sometimes the first few paragraphs, whether they can safely entrust their imaginations and emotions to the writer's skill and follow willingly wherever the story takes them.

A skillful writer cultivates this kind of trust in the reader by first setting up characters with emotionally-evocative traits as detailed in the previous chapters. Then the writer plants cues validating the reader's anticipated emotional response to those traits. These cues act like subliminal signposts to the reader, reassuring them they're on the same path as the author.

To plant an emotionally validating cue for the reader, first show a character demonstrating a certain positive or negative empathy trait. An example is Lucy in *While You Were Sleeping*, when she jumps on the train tracks to save a handsome stranger. The writers, Daniel G. Sullivan and Fredric LeBow, show the audience the Admiration Trait of courage in action.

Second, show another person in the story respond emotionally to that trait in the character. In *While You Were Sleeping*, the comatose man's family responds by placing their trust unreservedly in Lucy as a courageous hero who risked her own life to save their son. By allowing the Callaghan family to trust Lucy because of her courage, the writers subtly send the message to the audience it's okay for the viewer to trust Lucy, too.

It's as simple as cause and effect, or stimulus and response.

The character's rooting interest or empathy breaking trait is the cause or stimulus. Another character's emotional response is the effect that validates the reader's own feelings.

Of course, other characters in the story may have motivations influencing them to respond differently. An example in *While You Were Sleeping* is the comatose man's brother, Jack, the romantic hero of the story. While he's glad his brother is alive and will recover, his initial emotional response to Lucy is suspicion. Chiefly because he knows his brother so well, he senses all is not as it seems. A unity of feeling among all the characters is not necessary for the audience's emotional validation. The audience still trusts in Lucy, even when Jack does not. They only need a minimum of one character who honestly responds with the same feeling they felt the moment the character demonstrated a rooting interest (or empathy breaking) trait.

By maintaining this cause-and-effect emotional chain throughout the story, the writer nourishes the reader's faith in them as a storyteller in touch with genuine human emotions. Break the chain by forgetting to show either the proper stimulus or response, and the reader's confidence in the writer will spring a leak and rapidly drain away.

An example of broken trust with the writer might look something like this—

The hero and heroine crash their car and are stranded in the wilderness at night. The heroine jumps at every little noise, literally clings to the hero's coattail for every step, is so afraid she can't think of a single useful thing to do next, and when she twists her ankle breaks into hysterics. When the hero goes off to gather wood for a fire, she sits frozen with fear on a rock, and makes herself sick imagining all sorts of terrible things... These are all demonstrations of Empathy Breaking traits. As an emotional stimulus, the effect it has on the reader is impatience at best and scorn at worst.

Now suppose the hero returns with wood to build the fire, finds her panicked out of her mind, and responds emotionally with admiration for her courage and fortitude? The reader is likely to go, *Huh?* They'll wonder if the writer truly believes whining and panicking is courageous behavior worthy of respect. As the hero is the only other character around at the moment (other than an owl or squirrel), the reader is forced to accept the hero's response as the author's emotional cue. But because the hero's emotions do not validate the reader's, the cause-and-effect chain doesn't hold together. The reader's trust in the author snaps and breaks. Their emotional connection to the story falls apart as a result, and they're liable to close the book and leave it without wasting any more of their time.

Be aware that the validating character's emotional response often demonstrates an empathy trait of its own in action. So while the reader receives validation for how they feel toward Character A's actions via the conduit of Character B's feelings, Character B's response creates its own emotional stimulus in the reader, as well. An example is Patricia Veryan's historical romance *Ask Me No Questions*. The aloof hero has made the heroine feel coldly unwelcome as a guest worker on his father's estate, and when she accidentally damages the estate's prized lawn, she braces for a harsh rebuke. Instead, the hero unexpectedly covers for her with his excitable father, taking the blame upon himself. This Likability Trait not only endears him to the reader, but also to the heroine, who consequently demonstrates a Likability Trait of her own by experiencing a change of heart about him.

Chapter Ten discussed the importance of establishing a dominant rooting interest category for the character. This decision pays off exponentially when it comes to validating the reader's emotional response. The character becomes so closely identified with the emotion those traits evoke, that they essentially become a Tension Character, or a Likability Character, or an Admiration Character. A powerful phenomenon then occurs subconsciously within the reader. Because they feel certain emotions so strongly toward that character, they judge other people in the story based on those people's emotional responses to the character.

An example is Raymond "Red" Reddington, the protagonist in TV's hit crime drama *The Blacklist*. Red is a classic Admiration Character. He's the mastermind of all criminal masterminds. A consummate man of mystery, he's the go-to man when anyone needs difficult-to-find answers or help getting out of trouble. He's confident, but never prideful. He's patient and self-controlled, capable of laying out intricate preparations years in advance. Cautious about his personal life, he's nevertheless devoted to a few close friends and willing to protect FBI profiler Lizzie Keen literally at all costs, even at the risk of his own life. The audience trusts Red implicitly. They trust Lizzie *because* she trusts Red, too. And they distrust anyone who *doesn't* trust Red because their emotional response invalidates the audience's own feelings toward the character.

Admiration Characters can become such a compelling presence in the story, that their threatened or sudden absence can knock the struts out from under the reader and other characters. In J.R.R. Tolkien's *The*

Hobbit and *The Lord of the Rings* trilogy, Gandalf the Gray is an Admiration Character whom others look up to as their confidence of survival and eventual success. When he bids farewell to Bilbo and the dwarves at the edge of Mirkwood Forest, the company of treasure hunters are cast into utter despair and grief. How can they possibly make it without him? They already knew the journey would be hazardous and difficult, but without Gandalf it seems impossible. Similar feelings descend on the Fellowship after Gandalf is lost in the Mines of Moria in *The Fellowship of the Ring,* and the reader wonders how any of them can make it without Gandalf's sure hand guiding them?

An example of a different type comes from the supporting love interest in the Kdrama *City Hunter*. Presidential bodyguard Kim Nana is a classic Likability Character. Devoted to her beloved father, she still suffers guilt for the accident that left him in a coma for the past decade. She gets along great with kids, and is quick to defend anyone being bullied. Her perpetual cheerful outlook springs from an unshakable determination to face life unflinchingly, and when she recognizes she's been too hasty judging someone, she's humble enough to change her mind and own up to it. Within the first five minutes onscreen, the audience likes Kim Nana so much that she instantly becomes the "heart" of the story. Later, when it seems she may die, for a few heartbreaking moments it feels as though the story's lifeblood is draining away, too. The audience likes the protagonist-hero all the more *because* from the very beginning he likes Kim Nana so very much. And they dislike any character who dislikes Kim Nana or doesn't recognize how special she is.

Likability Characters have the amazing ability, just by being themselves, to inspire others to be better people and strive to make a better life for themselves. They are a beacon shining warmly in the darkness for those floundering in a cold sea of shame or self-destruction. In TV's

Person of Interest, NYPD homicide Detective Jocelyn Carter is a Likability Character who helps redeem the protagonist from slowly sliding into suicide and contributes to his transformation into a noble vigilante hero. When she's targeted for death by corrupt cops, the protagonist's moral compass is put in jeopardy. She's not only one of the main characters, she's the "heart" of the series, the reference point for everything right and wrong in the story's universe.

An earlier chapter already explored Dr. Richard Kimble in *The Fugitive* as a classic Tension Character. A victim of injustice when his testimony about his wife's murder is not believed, he's forced to repress his emotional pain over her loss in order to track down her killer. Injured, alone, hunted like an animal by the authorities, he experiences physical jeopardy over and over again. The audience worries about Kimble constantly, and hopes for his success. They worry about other characters who try to help him, and hope their assistance is successful. And they despair over anyone who doesn't care what happens to him, and suffer outrage at those who place him in additional danger.

Tension Characters make those around them feel stronger by unconsciously appealing to their protective instincts. Here's someone who deserves consolation, comfort, and support through life's unfair trials. That's why they are capable by their presence in a story of bringing out the best in others—or exposing the worst. In *Lassie Come Home*, a boy's financially-strapped family is forced to sell his beloved pet, a devoted collie, who makes an arduous journey against all odds to find her way back to his side. As Lassie crosses paths with other characters, her literal underdog status draws forth their true nature for the audience to behold. Will they utilize their sense of power over a suffering animal for goodness and mercy, or to take out repressed fear and hostility?

Examine the rooting interests and empathy breaking traits you've assigned to your character. For every trait, find at least one other person who either personally witnesses it or is directly impacted by it in some way. Validate the reader's emotional experience by matching that other character's emotional response to the emotion the trait is designed to evoke in the reader.

For example, Tension Traits evoke feelings like anxiety, worry, apprehension, anticipation, dread, or suspense in the reader. Likability Traits evoke sensations like approval, warmth, friendliness, understanding, agreeableness, or enchantment. Admiration Traits evoke emotions like trust, respect, esteem, appreciation, amazement, or surprise. So when a character's situation or behavior inspires the reader to experience any of these emotions, they need to know someone else in the story is worrying about, or liking, or admiring the character, too. That cues readers that they and the writer are in emotional sync and that it's okay to trust the author to take them on a satisfying fictional journey.

– Chapter Thirteen –

Darth Vader

Appeared in: *Star Wars* saga
Written by: George Lucas

Story: In a galaxy far, far away a farm boy, a princess, and a smuggler join forces in an unlikely friendship (and semi-love triangle) to fight for freedom alongside rebel forces against the overwhelming might of the evil Galactic Empire. As each pursue their own missions for the cause, they all must eventually cross swords with the tip of the enemy's spear: the legendary dark Jedi knight, Darth Vader.

Character: While the Galactic Empire's evil Emperor is suppose to be the primary villain in *Star Wars*, we all recognize the real power behind the story is Darth Vader. Even in the prequels filmed years after the initial trilogy, it's his complex history that's explored and the tragic trajectory of his character arc that's given detailed expression. Some sources suggest George Lucas drew inspiration for Darth Vader from Jesus in the Bible, which is highly ironic since he created a character widely regarded as one of the greatest villains of all time.

Tip #1 — **Mysteries and consequences.** If there's ever been a man of mystery, it's Darth Vader. Master practitioner of a mysterious religion, his past is shrouded in carefully guarded secrets that ultimately rock the lives and hearts of every major character in the series. The audience doesn't even know what he looks like for several films, though it hardly matters since his black-garbed presence radiates a powerful menace whenever he appears on screen. Like Chekhov's proverbial gun on the mantel, mysteries are like loaded weapons waiting to go off. The audience's curiosity demands each one pay off with consequences, and Darth Vader's pays off with some of the biggest physical and personal consequences in film history. Remember the one about a certain main character's true parentage?

Tip #2 — **It takes more than a scary costume to be truly scary.** The black cape, breathing mask, and Samurai helmet have become as iconic as the character himself. Just check out any *Star Wars* convention. While the all-black costume lends effective subliminal support to Darth Vader's menacing presence, his real power as a villain comes from the extent to which corruption has devoured his sense of humanity. Vengeance has taken the place of justice. Possession has eclipsed mercy and compassion. All the good that was in his soul has been reprogrammed for evil. A character who has lost or abandoned his connection to moral values of right and wrong necessary to guide powerful Admiration Traits is scary in the extreme. He's worse than a monster, who at least would be subject to pain. He's an implacable robot with the devil himself working the remote control.

Tip #3 — **Evil is contagious.** Genuine goodness in a character is inspirational, never pushy. But evil never gives up trying to snare others into its sticky web. Like a virus, it always searches for new hosts to infect with its dark power. This is Darth Vader's modus operandi. He uses his evil power to intimidate, compel, or tempt others to join their power with his for the dark side. Even though he may act like the Emperor's flunky sometimes, Darth Vader is never passive. Whether he's crushing a smart-mouthed stormtrooper's windpipe or coaxing Luke to betray the rebels, his ultimate purpose is to accrue more power for the forces of darkness. With the fate of the galaxy at stake, that's scary indeed!

Chapter Fourteen

Ebenezer Scrooge

Appeared in: *A Christmas Carol*
Written by: Charles Dickens

Story: A bitter old miser is visited on Christmas Eve by his late partner's ghost with a warning to immediately change his ways or else suffer eternal misery in the afterlife. Later that night three spirits take Scrooge on a journey into his past, present, and future, where he learns a new perspective on life, love, and generosity.

Character: First published in 1843, Charles Dickens' *A Christmas Carol* has remained perpetually in print to this day. It's popularity was instant and enduring, spawning numerous adaptations on stage, radio, and movies. This is in no small part thanks to its iconic protagonist, Scrooge, whose very name is a recognized synonym for miserliness. The incredible journey of this tight-fisted old sinner into a near saint of open-hearted generosity has inspired many real-life acts of goodwill toward men for generations.

Tip #1 — **Stakes characters.** While *A Christmas Carol* is all about Scrooge, early on Dickens introduces readers to two supporting characters whose fates are tied to the protagonist's. If Scrooge doesn't change into a better human being, it becomes abundantly clear that these two characters and those they care about will suffer miserably for his moral failure. Even if the reader has little if any rooting interest in Scrooge at the beginning, they can't help but root for his long-suffering clerk and unconditionally cheerful nephew. These personal stakes only deepen later on with the introduction of Tiny Tim. With so many cherished characters hanging in the balance, the reader is compelled to root for Scrooge's triumph over his own mean nature.

Tip #2 — **Capacity for change.** Few stories use flashbacks as creatively as *A Christmas Carol*. Instead of stagnant examinations of the past, they're transformed into vibrant forward drivers of the story as Scrooge's visit to his past becomes his present reality pressuring him to grow and mature. Perhaps these flashbacks' most essential service to the story is revealing Scrooge's capacity for good. While providing insight into why Scrooge is the way he is now, even sympathy for the neglected child he was, they also provide the reader with genuine hope he can change for the better. These formerly suppressed memories challenge his self-concept as a cold-hearted tightwad. Because readers are shown he was once a joyous and warmhearted soul, they can believe he's capable of becoming a joyous and warmhearted child-at-heart again—however great the odds against him.

Tip #3 — **Extreme jeopardy.** Marley's Ghost makes it abundantly clear to Scrooge he deserves what he's got coming to him. He's diligently forged every link in his own chain of torment. There is inarguable justice in the danger staring Scrooge in the face. Nevertheless, the extreme jeopardy represented by imminent and eternal damnation is so great, what reader can resist feeling tension for Scrooge's situation?

He faces the specter of death itself, and worse than death. He's in jeopardy of spending eternity in an agony of desperate, exhausting regret from which he will never find release.

Chapter Fifteen

James Bond

Appeared in: *Dr. No* and other stories
Written by: Ian Fleming

Story: A restful working holiday in Jamaica to investigate the disappearance of a MI6 station chief turns deadly for 007 when the trail leads him to an island haunted by a fire-breathing dragon. There he discovers a wealthy recluse working with hostile foreign powers to sabotage United States missile tests. Captured and tortured, Bond races against the tide to destroy Dr. No's underground complex.

Character: Described in Fleming's novels as a cold, ruthless version of musician/songwriter/actor Hoagy Carmichael, James Bond was originally written as the anonymous, uninteresting eye at the center of global espionage hurricanes. With the help of Sean Connery's dashing portrayal on screen in *Dr. No*, 007 became more than a plain reflection of exotic surroundings and international intrigue. The character himself became a superstar of sex appeal, glamor, and excitement. Accompanied by guns, gadgets, and girls galore, he carved an iconic niche in popular culture via movies, television, radio, comics, and post-Fleming novels for over sixty years.

Tip #1 — **Characters are fun when they have fun things to do and enjoy doing them.** Bond is not known for being an especially realistic, complex, or deeply dimensional character. But he sure is a lot of fun and presses all the right buttons for escapist adventure par excellence. Because he's not heavily associated with serious themes or weighty social issues, he offers a temporary relief from real life stresses. 007 never has to fix clogged plumbing or pay off a mortgage or try to lose twenty unwanted pounds. All of his rooting interest traits are demonstrated within the context of thrilling adventures the audience might like to experience (without getting hurt), like vacationing on a Caribbean paradise, fighting a mechanical fire-breathing dragon, or surviving an attack by a giant squid. Whatever Bond is doing, he does it with zest and enthusiasm for his work. Even while being tortured, he digs down past the pain and finds the inner fortitude for a quip at the villain's expense.

Tip #2 — **The bigger the stakes are the better, but remember to make them personal.** Bond is far too skilled and accomplished a resource for the government to waste on penny ante stakes. No matter how often the bad guys jeopardize the free world, the audience still gets a vicarious thrill watching 007 save the world over and over again. However, a key component of the audience's emotional engagement with the story comes from the personal stakes involved. What's at risk for the world's most famous secret agent emotionally if he fails to stop the villain? Sometimes it's his friends whom he's loyal to, like Quarrel, but most often it's his girl. Honey Rider isn't the great love of his life, but he does care about her enough to risk his own life to protect her from the villain's deadly scheme. More than just eye candy for teenage boys in the theatre, Bond girls play a lighthearted but nevertheless essential part in bonding the audience with the protagonist.

Tip #3 — **The strength of a story is it's antagonist.** Bond's villains are almost as iconic as he is. Whether it's Dr. No, Goldfinger, or Ernst Blofeld, any villain worthy of the role in a 007 story is always more than a match for our favorite spy. In many ways they're Bond's evil twin on heavy duty steroids: charming, diabolical, egomaniacal, display steely resolve, enjoy what they're doing, and are so skilled at killing they utilize demented and specialized methods of dispatching useless underlings or annoying opponents. It's precisely because Dr. No is so powerful and formidable that Bond comes off looking so good when he ultimately triumphs over him. The reason there is so much to admire about James Bond, despite his many tragic failings as a human being (or, God forbid, role model), is that even when confronted by overwhelming pressure or temptation to turn aside from good to evil, he's ultimately incorruptible. But it often takes a very corrupt madman for the audience to discover it.

– Chapter Sixteen –

Katniss Everdeen

Appeared in: *The Hunger Games* trilogy
Written by: Suzanne Collins

Story: In a dystopian future, a teenage girl volunteers to take her sister's place in a government-mandated gladiatorial death match staged as a TV reality show. Her teammate is a boy who cherishes an unrequited love for her, though according to the rules of the Game only one champion is allowed to walk away alive. To save herself and her own humanity, she must learn to surrender the emotional armor she's relied on and embrace a reckless hope... and an impossible love.

Character: While not the first kick-ass heroine ever created, Katniss quickly took the number one slot on many "Favorite Kick-Ass Heroines" lists worldwide when *The Hunger Games* was published in 2008. The series had over 24 million copies in print before the first movie adaptation was later released in 2012, and the protagonist has inspired everything from hairstyles to baby/pet names to a renewed interest in archery for kids. Katniss has all the requisite dictionary attributes of the type: forceful, vigorous, aggressive. But what makes her stand out from the pack is her core motivation: she's driven to protect those she loves at all costs, even if it means setting the world of Panem on fire.

Tip #1 — **The tougher the shell, the softer inside.** Kick-ass heroines may be hard as nails on the outside in order to survive in a rugged world, but inside they must have a soft heart capable of being easily touched. Ironically, that's usually why they're so defensive. More than anyone else, they're aware that their ability to genuinely and deeply care about someone is their greatest vulnerability. The first page in *The Hunger Games* reveals Katniss' years-earlier pragmatic attempt to drown a starving kitten she couldn't afford to feed. But this sure-fire Empathy Breaker is immediately rescued from irredeemability by the fact she couldn't go through with it because of her beloved baby sister's pleas and tears. Her love for Prim is her soft spot, her moral engine that drives her decisions at several key turning points in the story.

Tip #2 — **It's a dangerous world to live in, but somebody's got to.** Kick-ass heroines live in an inherently dangerous world. If they weren't born with that awareness, they learned it early on and determined with gritted teeth to rise to the occasion. From the first page of *The Hunger Games* to the last, the threat of danger is ever-present. When it isn't stalking Katniss from the bushes, it's snapping right at her throat. The difference between kick-ass heroines and mere mortals is that heroines like Katniss are grimly intimate with the dark side of life. Thus when bad things happen, they aren't taken totally unawares like "normal" people who may freeze in shock. They pay shorter attention than most to common human responses like denial, delay, and deliberation, and move on quickly to the decisive action necessary for survival. When Prim's name is called as a Tribute, Katniss doesn't waste hours or days mulling over what to do. She spends one scant page absorbing the horror of the situation and instinctively springs into action.

Tip #3 — **It takes more than kicking ass to make a kick-ass heroine.** Despite their aggressive reputation and well-honed martial skills, kick-ass heroines don't go around trying to start fights. Katniss actually spends half of the first book running and hiding, trying to *avoid* having to fight, until she's literally trapped up a tree with nowhere to go. Only when all other options are stripped away and she's denied any other recourse does she turn around and take the battle to the enemy. It's difficult for readers to admire reckless hotheads who unnecessarily court disaster for the juvenile thrill of letting off some steam. That's why successful kick-ass heroines always fight smarter first, before having to fight harder. They understand better than most the real consequences of failure could mean death (for themselves or others), so they wisely choose their confrontations only when strategically necessary or given absolutely no other choice.

Chapter Seventeen

Lee Yoon-sung, Kim Nana, & Lee Jin-pyo

Appeared in: *City Hunter*
Written by: Hwang Eun-kyung, Choi Soo-jin

Story: South Korean presidential bodyguard Lee Jin-pyo is betrayed by his government and left for dead during a top secret mission. Vowing revenge, he raises another man's son as his own, ruthlessly molding Lee Yoon-sung into his own secret weapon against the five corrupt officials responsible for the murders of his men. But as Yoon-sung falls in love with Blue House bodyguard Kim Nana, he fights to end the bloodshed fueling his foster father's terrible master plan.

Characters: Loosely based on the internationally bestselling Japanese manga series by Tsukasa Hojo, this original Korean drama production captured a whole new market of devoted fans worldwide with its "perfect combination of action and heart" (Dramabeans). Brilliantly written from beginning to end with pitch-perfect tone, pacing, and structure, everything works together so seamlessly it's difficult to point out one element as superior to the rest. But like every outstanding story, ultimately it's the characters in all their multifaceted complexity, richness and depth that propel *City Hunter* to a place of high honor in the hearts of the audience. Wisely departing from its source material, in which the protagonist was a lecherous pervert calloused to genuine devotion, the writers instead crafted a fresh central character whose dynamic power and charisma is balanced with hard-won maturity and almost childlike hope.

Tip #1 — **Antagonists are on a journey, too.** The writers do an incredible job of juggling several powerful villains, but the primary antagonist—the only one bent on personally crushing Yoon-sung's soul—is his foster father, Jin-pyo. As menacing and evil as he is, he is far from a static bad guy. He begins the story as a heroic and skilled soldier who survives a horrific betrayal only because his best friend sacrifices himself, dying in Jin-pyo's arms. Because these powerful Tension and Likability Traits bond the audience to him right away, viewers are emotionally invested in his outcome, even when they eventually can no longer root for him to succeed. The course of revenge he sets for himself takes him on an increasingly dark path, and to stay true to his chosen course, he diligently attempts to suffocate any potential weaknesses—like love and devotion—that might undermine his plans. Every time he pressures Yoon-sung to embrace bloodlust, Yoon-sung challenges Jin-pyo to turn back to love and justice before it's too late. This dynamic push-pull energizes both men's character arcs all the way until the heartrending conclusion.

Tip #2 — **Alter egos are cool, but it's the character behind the mask that makes the reader's heart beat.** Yoon-sung is a vigilante hero in the best tradition of Batman, the Lone Ranger, and the Scarlet Pimpernel. Ordinary men, extraordinarily skilled, forced to conceal their real identity behind a mask while deceiving the world with a barefaced illusion. When characters live part of the story undercover, it's important to show readers the real them first. That's who the reader has to emotionally bond with, because it's the real them that carries the personal stakes in the story, not the alter ego. That's why Yoon-sung's internal goal, conflict, and motivation are all carefully set up in the first episode. Long before he becomes the City Hunter, the audience witnesses his mistreatment as a child, his repressed pain and longing for parental affection, his loneliness, his instinctive defense of the helpless and victimized, his willingness to risk his life for another, his compassion, and his protectiveness of those he cherishes. These early Likability and Tension Traits invest a touching vulnerability in the character even as he develops into an admired dispenser of justice the audience unreservedly trusts to save the day. On the rare occasions he ever loses a fight it's because he either succeeds too well or the bad guys' well-prepared bag of dirty tricks finally pays off. It's never because he makes foolish mistakes or suddenly and inexplicably becomes less skillful and resourceful.

Tip #3 — **When the going gets tough, the tough need a soft spot.**
While protagonist Yoon-sung is loaded with Admiration Traits (courageous, skilled, powerful, protective, big picture, confident, just, mysterious, cultured, attractive, etc...), his romantic interest Kim Nana is richly endowed with Likability Traits. These two are perfectly matched, because while Yoon-sung often acts cold, gruff, and haughty (partly to protect others by holding them at a distance, partly because of his harsh upbringing), the audience still likes him because he sincerely adores the sweetly spunky Kim Nana. First glimpsed simultaneously by the audience and Yoon-sung in a cherished photograph, Kim Nana becomes the embodiment of his fragile dreams for a normal life apart from his foster father's violent quest. When she finally steps onto the scene in person, she's packed with such strong back-to-back Likability

Traits with just the right dash of Tension and Admiration Traits, that the audience immediately and irrevocably falls in love with her. It's no wonder Yoon-sung does, too.

Chapter Eighteen

Scarlett O'Hara

Appeared in: *Gone With the Wind*

Written by: Margaret Mitchell

Story: A spoiled Georgia belle fights to survive and triumph amid the harsh brutalities of the American Civil War and Reconstruction. Traumatized by hardship, poverty, and loss, she jettisons the finer qualities of honor, kindness, and decency in her drive to "never go hungry again" and to ensnare the married man who personifies a chivalrous but dying era. Supporting her through it all is the fragile woman she desperately scorns yet whose inner strength she relies upon, and the dashing rake who craves her heart and soul while never daring to reveal the true depths of his love.

Character: A rose by any other name may smell as sweet, but there's no doubt the heroine of *Gone With the Wind* just wouldn't resonate as powerfully with readers if she'd been Pansy O'Hara. This is one of those occasions where a bold, unconventional name was necessary to express the essence of a bold, unconventional character. The quintessential survivor, Scarlett embodies the story's overriding theme with a gritted-teeth determination to live free or die trying. Her motto, "I'll think of it all tomorrow… After all, tomorrow is another day," is a promise to herself to endure today's trauma and live to see a new day.

Tip #1 — **Gumption.** That's how Margaret Mitchell described the intangible quality that's the mark of triumphant survivors in any catastrophe. It's a potent amalgamation of certain Admiration Traits. While Scarlett is persistent, shrewd, and confident to the point of vanity, she's also fiercely protective of the people she cares about and the home she loves above everything and everyone else. She'll work her fingers to the bone or burn her reputation to ashes if necessary to feed them and save Tara from carpetbaggers. The ability to comprehend the big picture fuels her undimmed initiative to grab opportunity with both hands. Though her methods leave many lives wrecked in her wake and numerous characters hate the ground she walks on, no one can help respecting the backbone and courage she demonstrates surviving war and enemy occupation.

Tip #2 — **Blind spots and fatal flaws.** While Scarlett's skilled at ruthlessly converting her ambitions into reality, she's a tragically flawed character when it comes to personal relationships. While she can instinctively take measure of the forest, she's often blind to the individual trees until a limb wallops her right in the face. This happens over and over again throughout the story, such as when she returns home and is confronted with her father's pitiful incapacity to run Tara, or when she realizes at Melanie's deathbed how she depended on the fragile woman and doesn't really love Ashley, or when she rushes belatedly to Rhett's side with her confession of love. In every case the truth was staring her in the face all along, but she didn't realize it until too late. In many ways Scarlett is a larger-than-life force of nature, but blinders of selfish immaturity narrow her vision so acutely that the reader can't help but taste counterbalancing emotions of frustration and pity. It's the flavor of a complex character that readers and audiences haven't been able to get enough of for over seventy-five years.

Tip #3 — **Action scenes have meaning when intensely personal stakes are involved.** One of the most memorable scenes in the book and movie is the burning of Atlanta, when Rhett helps Scarlett escape with Melanie, Prissy, and the baby. It's a big set piece, literally aflame with tension and danger. But like any successful action sequence, the motivation for the characters' presence and participation is deeply personal, making the gunfire and explosions much greater than the sum of their parts. Built into the foundation of all this tension is a Likability Trait that rounds out Scarlett's character with riveting internal conflict and dimension. She stays in harm's way only because she promised Ashley she'd look after Melanie. Even though she hates Melanie, even though she wishes Melanie were dead so she could claim Ashley for herself, even though it means risking her own life and sanity amid the terror of Sherman's bombing—she keeps her word.

– Chapter Nineteen –

Sherlock Holmes

Appeared in: *A Study in Scarlet* and other stories
Written by: Sir Arthur Conan Doyle

Story: Recovering from war wounds received in Afghanistan, Dr. John Watson moves into 221B Baker Street with consulting detective Sherlock Holmes. At first curious then skeptical about his roommate's brilliant observation and deductive abilities, Watson winds up urging his new friend to take up a case whose "scarlet thread of murder" unravels a 40-year-old tapestry of lost love, kidnapping, and revenge.

Character: Although not the first detective ever enshrined in fiction or film, Sherlock Holmes inspired many who followed: Hercule Poirot, Nero Wolfe, Perry Mason, Adrian Monk, and even medical-sleuth Dr. Gregory House, M.D., to name a few. Beyond the original four novels and 56 short stories penned by Doyle, Holmes has enjoyed undying popularity on radio, film, television, comics, and non-canonical works. He is literally the character whom readers refuse to let die, as demonstrated when fans demanded Doyle bring back the famous sleuth after killing him off in *The Final Problem*.

Tip #1 — **Genuine eccentrics aren't eccentric to be weird, they're just passionate.** Sherlock Holmes is an eccentric, no doubt about that. But his unconventional interests and slightly strange be-havior aren't merely quirks designed to make him appear different from other characters. His eccentricity is fueled by raw, unadulterated passion to be the best at what he does. He doesn't care what people think of him otherwise, so long as they respect and admire his contri-bution to his field. This is how he's first introduced to readers and the narrator: laughing, his face shining with enthusiasm and eagerness, as delighted with the results of a forensics experiment as a kid with a shiny new toy. Passion is riveting to behold on the page or screen. Readers share Watson's deepening curiosity about this mysterious man who couldn't care less about basic astronomy, yet who spends weeks at a time intensively expanding his already profound understanding of chemistry.

Tip #2 — **Give the character's consuming passion a practical application in the plot.** Sherlock Holmes' obsession for information and detailed analysis has a highly practical value in the story. If his ec-centricities possessed no practical application, he'd simply look like an oddball dashing about with his tape measure and large round magnify-ing glass. Instead he appears brilliant, even foresightful for having ac-cumulated exactly the skills and knowledge necessary for the peculiar tasks at hand. At critical moments his skills enable him to deduce the unknown suspect's height, age, cigar brand, and even the length of his fingernails. But as practical as Holmes's purposes invariably are, the character benefits from remaining somewhat a man of mystery, his methods ultimately as guarded as a magician's cleverest tricks.

Tip #3 — **Somebody values the character's unique skills.** In *A Study in Scarlet*, Scotland Yard rivals Lestrade and Gregson seek out Holmes's assistance precisely because of his eccentric mastery of detection. Though each are deemed the best of a conventional lot and both salivate over claiming credit for solving crimes, they nevertheless recognize and value Holmes's amazing ability to ferret out unseen keys to complex cases. That other characters find it important Holmes can reliably translate random details into hard evidence, cues the reader to the real worth of Holmes's unusual skill set. It doesn't exist as a mere ploy to amuse the reader. In the story world it has important value own to other characters with something of their own at stake. For Lestrade and Gregson, it's the kind of glory that can advance their careers. For Watson, it's a deeper understanding of his companion and an awakening to a new purpose in life.

Chapter Twenty

Emotional Bonding Checklist

The following checklist represents all the exercises found in this book, compiled into one convenient reference. If you've been following along with the exercises, then you already have everything you need to fill it out. Otherwise, use it to capture flashes of inspiration or to help organize developmental notes.

Story Title:

Character's Name:
Relevant cultural, religious, or historical significance:

Role (*protagonist, antagonist, romantic interest, mentor, sidekick, etc.*):

CHARACTER SNAPSHOT

Male or female:
Attitudes / values about gender:

Age:
Attitudes / values about age:

Job / Hobbies:
Attitudes / values about job and hobbies:

Physical appearance:
Attitudes / values about physical appearance:

Positive Personality Trait #1:
Tags…
Physical detail:
Skill:
Dialogue:
Behavior:
Quirk:

Positive Personality Trait #2:
Tags…
Physical detail:
Skill:
Dialogue:
Behavior:
Quirk:

Positive Personality Trait #3:
Tags…
Physical detail:
Skill:
Dialogue:
Behavior:
Quirk:

Negative Personality Trait:
Tags…
Physical detail:
Skill:
Dialogue:
Behavior:
Quirk:

Backstory summary paragraph (*focus on fears, beliefs, worldview, relationships*):

BUILD THE STORY

Character's story-length external goal:

Character's motivation for goal:

Character's plan for achieving goal:

How their flaw makes the plan fail:

Character's new and improved plan:

Central story question (*"Will [character] be able to [carry out plan] in spite of [opposition]?"*):

Physical stakes (*best possible outcome versus worst possible outcome*):

Emotional stakes (*gain or loss relative to important relationship involved*):

Defining backstory event binding character to present stakes:

What does the character attempt to do that has either *never been done before, few have succeeded at,* or is *prohibited by some authority*?

Courage sentence:

CHOOSE EMPATHY TRAITS

Story genre:

Primary emotional experience this genre delivers to readers (*tension, warmth, thrills, etc.*):

Empathy traits required because of the plot:

Empathy traits required because of the character's internal arc:

Empathy traits associated with the story's theme:

Write a brief step-outline of plot events, grouped by Empathy Traits.
Total number of events associated with Tension Traits:
Total number of events associated with Likability Traits:
Total number of events associated with Admiration Traits:
Primary rooting interest category:

Character's primary flaw:

Empathy Breaker Traits demonstrating his or her flaw—
Tension/Horror:
Likability/Repulsion:
Admiration/Scorn:

How are the Empathy Breaker Traits redeemed?
Tension/Horror:
Likability/Repulsion:
Admiration/Scorn:

Review the step-outline of the plot and the empathy breaking traits above.
For each trait, list which other character in the story validates the reader's
anticipated emotional response:

Texts Cited

Bickham, Jack M. *Writing and Selling Your Novel.* Cincinnati: Writer's Digest Books, 1996. Print.

Dixon, Debra. *Goal, Motivation, and Conflict: the Building Blocks of Good Fiction.* Memphis: Gryphon Books for Writers, 1996. Print.

Edson, Eric. *The Story Solution.* Studio City: Michael Wiese Productions, 2011. Print.

Iglesias, Karl. *Writing for Emotional Impact.* Livermore: WingSpan Press, 2005. Print.

James Wray and Ulf Stabe (2007-02-04). "Scorsese takes top DGA honors." *Monsters and Critics.* Retrieved 2014-07-09.

Maass, Donald. *The Fire in Fiction.* Cincinnati: Writer's Digest Books, 2009. Print.

Sokoloff, Alexandra. *Writing Love: Screenwriting Tricks for Authors II.* 2011. Digital.

St. John, Cheryl. *Writing with Emotion, Tension, and Conflict.* Blue Ash: Writer's Digest Books, 2013. Print.

Swain, Dwight V. *Techniques of the Selling Writer.* Norman: University of Oklahoma Press, 1965. Print.

TRANSFORM YOUR FAVORITE NOVEL INTO
YOUR PERSONAL WRITING COACH

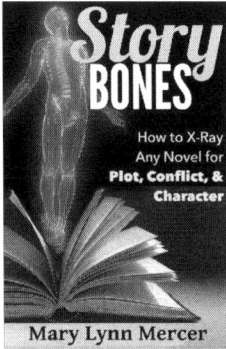

Have you ever run up against a story problem that made you want to beat your head against a wall, wishing for a way to correctly diagnose and treat it? Is a manuscript lying paralyzed in a desk drawer somewhere, waiting for a broken conflict to be mended? Do you long to line your characters up in front of an X-ray machine so you can peer inside them?

Maybe it's time to call in a consulting team of "specialists," experts in their field who've been there, done that, and have the published novels (and reader fan base) to prove it. Consider your favorite authors as doctors who, for the price of their novels, can be called at any time to provide insights into a difficult case.

This book will empower you to—

- Analyze any novel, movie, or television episode for insights into plot, conflict, and character development.
- Track the four throughlines that make engaging stories multidimensional.
- Master the eight sequences and turning point events that infuse stories with meaningful change.
- Identify the eight archetypes that "show, don't tell" theme.
- Recognize the three different types of character arcs and nine unique personalities that define character growth.
- Understand the five empathy elements that win reader identification.

Enjoy examples drawn from modern bestsellers and timeless classics. BONUS: in-depth analyses of J.R.R. Tolkien's fantasy novel, The Hobbit, and the blockbuster romantic comedy, While You Were Sleeping. Includes original, easy-to-understand diagrams and helpful charts available as handy printable versions online.

Available now in Kindle edition and in print on Amazon and other booksellers.

ISBN: 0-615-94367-5   ISBN-13: 978-0-615-94367-1

CRAFT AN EMOTIONALLY CHARGED STORY THAT KEEPS READERS TURNING PAGES

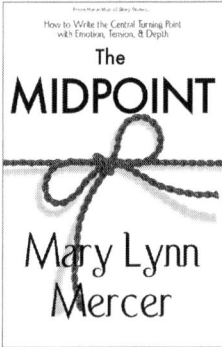

Have you ever started writing a story, feeling full of inspiration and enthusiasm, only to lose direction somewhere in the middle?

Grab hold of a bright lifeline for writers trekking across their novel's swampy middle. Like Ariadne's thread guiding Theseus through the treacherous labyrinth, there exists a scarlet cord to help successfully navigate from beginning to end.

Much more than a "plot point" to energize pacing, the Midpoint is the central nervous system controlling the entire story. Mastering the Midpoint helps writers survive and thrive in the Everglades of the middle. Rediscover the spark in your story by learning how to--

- Design a Midpoint with depth by crafting realistic, multi-dimensional character flaws that resonate emotionally with readers.

- Strategically position the Midpoint at the apex of a simple four-step story structure that reflects realistic human self-improvement.

- Connect the three key events (the Midpoint is one of them!) in every story that are absolutely vital to creating escalating tension.

- Translate the eight essential functions of the Midpoint into specific beats and scenes reflecting your unique creative vision.

- Apply three quick and easy "tools" to craft Midpoints with maximum dramatic impact.

Ignite your creativity while enjoying dozens of examples from novels, television, and movies. Fantasy, inspirational, mystery, science fiction, western, young adult, romantic suspense, and contemporary/historical romance--every genre contributes valuable insights.

Available now in Kindle edition and in print on Amazon and other booksellers.

ISBN: 0-692-23862-X   ISBN-13: 978-0-692-23862-2